COOKIN' WITH CORKY'S

Dig in with family and friends from Memphis' legendary Bar-B-Q joint!

Jimmy Stovall

with **Andy Woodman** *and* **Barry Pelts**

Favorite Recipes® Press

TABLE OF CONTENTS

DEAR READERS,

It is with great joy and pride that
I present to you *Cookin' with Corky's:
Dig in with Family and Friends from
Memphis' Legendary BBQ joint*! This book
has been years in the making—you could say
since 1984, when Corky's first opened its doors
and so many of the people who contributed to this
book became involved with the restaurant that has
become such an integral part of my family and my life.

You'll see over and over in these pages that we call the people of
Corky's family. This is not just corporate jive talk. This is how we feel.
I hope that as you read this book and, more importantly, cook and taste
from this book, that you will come to love the Corky's family as much
as I do. We're quite a bunch and we love us some lip-smacking good
cooking. Whether you come visit us at our restaurants, order our
barbecue through QVC or our website, or master your own smoker
at home, I wish you the great,
good joy that barbecue can
bring to any table.

Eat well, live long, and
prosper! *(And add extra
sauce if necessary.)*

Yours,

Donald Pelts

Don Pelts

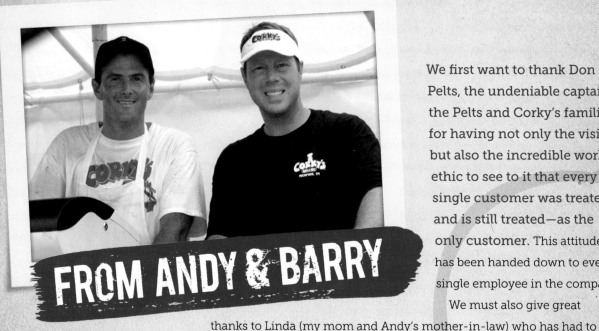

FROM ANDY & BARRY

We first want to thank Don Pelts, the undeniable captain of the Pelts and Corky's families, for having not only the vision, but also the incredible work ethic to see to it that every single customer was treated—and is still treated—as the only customer. This attitude has been handed down to every single employee in the company. We must also give great thanks to Linda (my mom and Andy's mother-in-law) who has had to live and breathe Corky's, Corky's, Corky's, 24-7 for almost 30 years! Similar kudos to our wives, Billie Pelts and Tricia Woodman. Our family's blood runs barbecue, and these women have stayed true to the cause, whatever Corky's shenanigans we came up with. To our children, Zachary, Brandon, Josh, Emma, and Zoe: we go to work every day in the hopes that we are creating a business that will be around for you long after we are gone. We built Corky's for you; we did this book for you. May you have as much fun cooking from it as we've had creating it.

This book would in no way have been possible without our fellow author, Jimmy Stovall, and our cookbook test-kitchen manager, Carol Sweeney, both key members of the daily Corky's team. Thank you for extending yourself well beyond your job description duties. We want to recognize, too, Amir Abdol, Joel Storck, Robbie Levine, and Bonnie Phifer. We always feel good knowing that you're running the ship, and we couldn't ask for more talented or loyal captains.

To Sheila Thomas with Favorite Recipes Press, thank you for having the vision for this book and the persistence to make it happen. We love the team you brought on—Martha Hopkins for her way with the written word, Julia Rutland, who can prop and style a photo shoot better than anyone I know, Jay Adkins, whose photographs make me hungry every time I look at them, and Randall Lockridge, whose graphic design talents brought the recipes and story of Corky's to life on every page of this book. Thank you all for making us look so good.

To every single employee: You are a part of the puzzle that has made Corky's what we are today. Don's vision is nothing without you, and we thank you for bringing Corky's a consistency and liveliness day in and day out.

Finally, to each and every customer who has enjoyed our barbecue all these years: Thank you so much! We say this from the bottom of our hearts. We know you have so many choices to experience world class barbecue in this great pork mecca of Memphis, Tennessee. But you, dear customers, have chosen us. We are humbled and grateful.

FROM JIMMY

My first thanks goes to QVC and all the folks who buy our barbecue each week. After years on the air, QVC feels like home. Thank you for buying this cookbook. I can guarantee you this: you won't be at a loss for sides for that rack of ribs again. To Lauren and Christina, who have believed in our product since day one. I'll make you nachos the next time I'm on campus. And to all the QVC hosts I work with. Thank you for making me look good and sound funny. Your job is much harder than it looks; you make mine easy.

To Lucy, my incomparable wife, who has allowed more random guests and impromptu BBQs at our house this summer than any wife should tolerate. To my kids, for being willing helpers for all these cookouts and photo shoots—especially JT, who ate watermelon and acted like he liked it, all in the name of "getting the shot."

A hearty thank you as well to our friends and colleagues who came to these aforementioned parties, submitting secret family recipes and bringing potluck portions so we could all try their homemade specialties. I have gained 10 pounds. Thank you.

Carol Sweeney and Joel Storck co-win the most indispensable award. Carol's test kitchen ran recipe after recipe through the ringer until it was something she'd be proud to serve anywhere. Joel runs our USDA distribution facility in Memphis and makes sure we always have exactly what we need in stock for our QVC customers. Thanks, too, to all the other Corky's employees who have gone above and beyond in helping us get this book together—Jan, Bonnie, Geneva, and all the others. As usual, we could not have pulled this off without the Corky's team working like the well-oiled machine that we are. Another job well done!

They were tender, meaty, with the perfect tangy sauce.

"Aah, you're partially right," *replied Annette.* "Corky's, yes. But the dry ribs. I'd never had them before. I think I've found rib nirvana."

— An excerpt from a Southern Living article on two food writers' quest for the best ribs in Memphis. Corky's won.

Corky's HISTORY

That's right. Corky's won. And I'm more than happy to toot our horn. But according to my dad, Don Pelts—and also the founder of Corky's—it's not about the food. I love our ribs, but I have to agree with him: It's about the service and the experience and the family of Corky's, the family of barbecue, the family of Memphis.

Here in Memphis, barbecue is a way of life. It's hard to explain to outsiders just how much smoked pork a town can bear. (A lot, to put it mildly. At Corky's alone, we go through nearly 5 million pounds of 'cue a year here.) The city hosts the largest BBQ fest in the world, the Memphis in May World Championship Barbecue Cooking Contest. More than 250 teams from 21 states and several countries compete for the coveted World Championship title. Memphis has more than 125 barbecue-only restaurants—nevermind all the places that serve ribs or pork on their menu.

9

Moms are as likely to pick up barbecue for a weeknight family dinner as chicken nuggets, and friends are just as likely to watch University of Memphis basketball over a slab of ribs as a slice of pizza. And that's just everyday eating. For holidays and family feasts, barbecue is our default, our must-have, our tried-and-true.

That's probably why my father first decided to open a barbecue joint back in 1972. His own father was getting out of the family furniture business and told my dad, "Don, you got to figure out something to do." So he did what no one in his right mind would do. He bought The Public Eye, a bar that served barbecue in Midtown Memphis. Without one shred of bar or restaurant experience.

If you know my dad, though, you know he's a natural in the restaurant business. You know that he knows everyone or wants to know everyone and even if he doesn't know you at all, he acts like he's known you forever. If you're eating his food, then you are his friend and his guest, and he's going to make sure you are treated *just right*.

The Public Eye, though, was a bar that served barbecue, not a barbecue joint that served alcohol. There's a crucial difference, in that one requires you to boot out drunks at 1 am and clean up their messes. The other has you serving sauce-stained meat that any soul would be happy to eat, along with a few cold ones to wash everything down. Crazy-time bar versus happy-time restaurant. For my dad, happy time was going to win this showdown, so he kept his eyes open for a fresh opportunity.

Opportunity appeared in the unlikely form of 5259 Poplar Avenue. If you were to look at a map of present-day Memphis, Tennessee, you'd see that this address sits smack dab in the heart of the city. It's an area of town called East Memphis that, at one point, was the eastern burbs of the town. No more. It is the city center, and Poplar Avenue is the lifeline that runs from downtown and the Mississippi River all the way out to the farthest suburb of Collierville.

The building he found was flanked by Krystal (and their (in)famous steamed square hamburgers), Captain D's (with

5259 Poplar Ave, circa 1984

extra crispies for anyone who asked), and McDonald's. Around the corner was Danver's, a Memphis roast beef chain with off-the-hook burgers and perfectly broiled buns, and Pancho's Tacos, a local Mexican food chain so popular that Memphis babies were weaned onto solid food with their cheese dip, crispy beef tacos, and unduplicatable green sauce.

Ella at the drive thru

Maybe the fact that he was surrounded by drive-thrus gave him the inspiration he needed to put a drive-thru in a sit-down barbecue restaurant. Or maybe the fact that the building was only 3,000 square feet and could only seat 85 customers spurred him to add a revenue stream beyond this tiny footprint. Whatever the case, Corky's drive-thru became a stroke of brilliance.

It took almost a year for Memphians to understand. You can get a just-pulled pork sandwich topped with creamy crunchy cole slaw and BBQ sauce in the same time that it takes to get a steamed burger. You can get three racks of ribs, a barbecue and spaghetti plate, and pecan pie to go in three minutes flat, all from the comfort of your car. That's not news today, now that every national chain from Chili's to Outback has added take-out areas to their restaurants, but in 1984, this was news. (And let's be honest, the big guys still don't have drive-thrus. You have to get out of your car and walk inside for most of them.)

So somewhere early on, the city of Memphis began to understand what was happening down at Poplar Avenue and Estate: Good food fast for families and friends. Big order? No problem. Ever. They started turning to us for all their events—for college graduations and high school reunions, for company cookouts and corporate gifts, for birthday parties and get togethers. Whether we were seating a table for 12 in the restaurant or handing over an order for 1500 through the drive-through, Corky's barbecue was becoming woven into the fabric of Memphis, one bite of pork at a time.

Of course, Memphians love to spread the love of good barbecue, so they'd bring their guests to Corky's to experience what we mean when we say barbecue. (Hint to Texans: it's not beef.) The out-of-towners would, inevitably,

our first
catering truck!

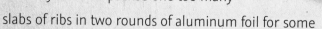

want to pack up some to-go containers with their leftovers for their family.

After my dad had packed one too many slabs of ribs in two rounds of aluminum foil for some businessman to carry on the plane home, we finally upgraded to custom styrofoam containers with dry ice. And then we added FedEx shipping for all those Southerners homesick for good 'cue up in the Yankee north or sunny California.

The orders started rolling in—5 a day grew to 25 a day grew to 2500 a day. Kroger and some other grocery stores started placing orders, too. One visit to our little home on Poplar Avenue, and you'll know there is no way that we could keep up with this kind of demand out of our Lilliputian kitchen. We expanded our production facility, but we made a commitment to ourselves early on. In short, if we couldn't maintain the quality that our customers knew and loved, from production through shipping and reheating at home, then we wouldn't be in the mail order business.

Somewhere in all this, around 1998, while we were up to our elbows in pulled pork and smoked ribs and mail-order, QVC came knocking. They had their own world of customers, and they wanted to introduce them to our meat. So again, we expanded our production facility, but stayed true to our original promise to ourselves: If we can't maintain the quality that our customers know and love, from production through shipping and reheating at home, then we won't be in the mail order business.

Today, we still use the exact same techniques my father first developed at the Public Eye and then moved over to Corky's at 5259 Poplar Avenue. Every single pork shoulder is smoked for 20 hours over a mix of charcoal and hickory. It is hand-pulled to order, no machine chopping in site. We flash freeze it, preserving quality and flavor until our customers are ready to serve it at home.

But like I said at the beginning, it isn't about the food. It really, really isn't. At the heart of Corky's are so many layers of families, with so many interconnections of cousins and nieces and couples that it's hard to keep things straight on our vast and elaborate family tree. The food becomes a simple vehicle for connection: The smoky pork brings us together, and our friendship keeps us together. (Though the buttered yeast rolls may play a part as well.)

Let's take my own family. First, there's Don, my dad. He's retired, but not really, if you know what I mean. He passed the business down to me and my brother-in-law, Andy Woodman. Andy is the numbers guy; I'm the marketing guy. And my dad, well, I suspect he'll just keep piping in until the very end—which is more than fine with all of us. You can't forget my mom, who made every single fudge pie and pecan pie that the restaurant served until 1991 when she finally said, "Enough, Don!" to the pies lining her kitchen counter. (He outsourced the job to a reputable

Young Don

Memphis bakery.) My sister, Tricia, and I both worked the restaurants as teenagers, and now my sister (Andy's wife) and my wife, Billie, run Simply Delicious, an upscale catering division for the restaurant.

Now, one tidbit about the Pelts family and our barbecue restaurant. We're Jewish. Better yet, our director of operations is Iranian. And the distribution of our employees, just like the distribution of Memphis, is an equal mix of black and white. Memphis is a town known for its deep-rooted racial history. Somehow, at Corky's we've managed to come to this as a family

that's in it together, for the long haul. Eighty percent of our managers have worked with us longer than 20 years. Our pit master, Robert Moye, worked with my father at the Public Eye. So did Joe Lee Johnson and Robbie Levine, AC Jackson, and Larry Eason. We have numerous multi-generational families working here. It starts

Chief Pitmaster Robert Moye and Melissa Massey

Legendary servers at Poplar. Clockwise from top left: Laetitia, Brian, Karla, Katie, Ann, Louise, and AC

13

Andy, Don, and Barry

with Pitmaster and Grandfather Robert Moye and his grandson, Scooter. Jimmy, whom you may know from QVC (not to mention our co-author and the mastermind behind this fabulous cookbook), met and married Lucy when they were both waiting tables. Lucy's brother Eddie is a manager. The list goes on, weaving its way through extended family trees and friend connections, with all roads leading right back to Corky's.

Other companies pride themselves on their lack of nepotism. For us, nepotism is almost a requirement, and it's certainly encouraged. If one of your family members works for us, then that's a good enough voucher for you to join the team. Why not work with the people who are nearest and dearest to you? We love doing that, and we assume our employees do, too.

Our employees also know that no job is too small or base for anyone. When our employees see my 73 year-old dad hauling trash out to the dumpster, they know that he doesn't place himself above them. Everyone starts at the drive-thru here—whether you have a college degree or you were a restaurant manager at a national chain or this is your first job and you're 16 years old, you are going to start here. From this tiny little space we serve thousands of invaluable (and hungry!) customers. It's a microcosm of the restaurant itself, and it's a key training ground for understanding how Corky's works.

At the end of the day, life is simple here at Corky's. We aim to make good barbecue, day in, day out. We want to have happy, contented customers, day in, day out. And we want to cultivate a workplace that feels good to the people involved. If these three things happen, we all feel we've done our job. It's a quality of life thing, and that's the kind of thing we're into here at Corky's. If you're not doing what you love with the people you love, what does anything matter?

Barbecue makes Memphians feel good. It's not a food for solitary pursuits. Who eats a slab of ribs alone or slow-smokes 12 pounds of Boston Butt by themselves? This is the food of community, of family, of friends. It's messy, yummy, smoky, saucy, and meaty. This book is a collection of all our favorite sides to Corky's barbecue and helps us share the love of Memphis-style eats.

I suppose that's the heart of the reason we're doing this book. It's a culmination of all those foods we so love to eat with our Memphis barbecue. Heck, there's even a whole chapter devoted solely to beans and slaw. (These obligatory—and celebrated!—sides are our queso to tortilla chips, our ketchup to French fries, our peanut butter to jelly. Don't even think about skipping them.)

You'll find things to do with leftover pork, on the rare occasion that you have some. We pair it with grits in a cast-iron skillet, stuff it in cornbread, wrap it in tortillas, and put it on pizza. You'll find more uses for barbecue sauce than you could ever imagine, starting with the crowd-pleasing Black-and-Blue Chicken to my kids' favorite, The Cadillac of Bar-B-Q Pizza. These recipes come directly from our home—from my home, from our employees' homes, from our customers' homes—to yours. (When we asked our customers for their favorite recipes, they came in from more than 16 states across America.) These are the dishes we make when we come together for good times, and we hope they find a place in your family's repertoire, too.

We wrote this book for Memphians and for anyone who has the pleasure of enjoying any of our hometown pork. Even if you can't eat it here with us at Corky's, we can send it to you, or you can recreate your own Memphis-style 'cue from the comfort of your own backyard. Invite your friends for your own rendition of good Southern cooking. Dig in, we say. Pig out! Eat up! Just don't forget the wet wipes. Barbecue can get a little messy.

Barry Pelts

There are some places where pork gets its due, and Memphis is one. Opinions vary, but most piggy experts would put Memphis right up near the top as a BBQ mecca, alongside Lockhart and Kansas City. And you cannot talk BBQ without talking pork. You can keep your yardbird and your beef tips. To me, and to others I know, you spell barbeque P-O-R-K. One year the BBQ fest of Memphis used the slogan "make pork not war" for their 60's-era theme. You get the point. You got to have a plate of pork to call it BBQ in my presence. Otherwise, it is "grilled chicken with sauce" or "veal in spicy tomato paste" and many serve something called BBQ spaghetti, but none to me are BBQ if they don't begin and end with pork.

— West (fan from Miami Beach, FL)

BBQ, BAR-B-Q, BAR-B-QUE, BARBEQUE, BARBECUE

No matter how you spell it, barbecue guarantees two things: 1) There's gonna be some good eatin' going on. 2) There's gonna be some arguing going on. No one can agree how to spell it, much less cook it. And dare we even ask which meat? *(It's pork, by the way.)*

When Texas writes their next barbecue book, they are welcome to argue otherwise. This book, however, is Memphis turf, and we've got some porky standards to uphold. But is barbecue a method or a meat? A noun or a verb? When we use the term barbecue, assume that we're talking about a slow-cooked, smoky piece of pig.

Our barbecue is barbecued, a verb that implies low, slow cooking on a smoker. To grill, at least for the purposes of this book, implies cooking meats, seafood, and vegetables on a charcoal or gas grill, usually over a higher heat.

Centered around family and friends gathering together, cooking out is one of the South's favorite pastimes. Whether cooking out for you means tinkering with your smoke box in between beers with the guys, or turning the knob to high on your built-in, stainless steel behemoth, most everyone agrees that cooking out means fun. There is just something about food smoked or seared over an open flame that appeals to our senses, be it smoldering hardwoods or a quick summer supper that keeps the heat and mess out of the kitchen. So even if we're gonna fight about what to cook and how to cook it, no one's going to suffer when it comes time to eat.

Memphis is known for our world-famous barbecue. Hundreds of thousands of barbecue enthusiasts and pit masters

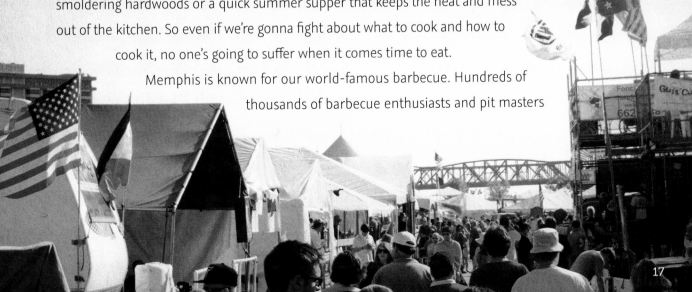

17

make the pilgrimage to Memphis each year to compete in the Memphis in May World Championship Barbecue Cooking Contest. The competition is fierce, the days are hot, and the beer lines are long. The 'cue is nothing short of legendary.

These blokes came from England to compete at Memphis in May!

We're best known in Memphis for dry ribs, and by that we mean pork ribs seasoned with a healthy coating of dry rub instead of the expected barbecue sauce. Each establishment has their own rub, always a top-secret mixture of dry spices and herbs that get massaged into the meat usually hours before smoking.

At Corky's, we've been serving wet and dry ribs for 28 years. Our customers can't seem to decide which is better, and neither can we. We barbecue the old fashioned way—the only way we know how—using real hickory wood and charcoal. Our pit masters smoke our pork shoulders for 24 hours, and they fire up the rib and chicken pits at 7 each morning.

Jack Holt working the ribs.

DIY Corky-Style Barbecue

Look for this icon throughout the book for grill-friendly recipes

All of our meats are available mail order, but you can make a mighty fine rendition on your own with a backyard smoker, a nice piece of meat, and plenty of seasoning.

We cook over wood and charcoal. Like barbecue itself, the use of woods is often regional. We like to use hickory, which is plentiful in the South, gives the best flavor, and burns low and slow. You will find mesquite the preferred wood in the Southwest, and alder in the Northwest.

A word of warning regardless of the species of hardwoods: make sure to use cured wood, never green woods, pressure treated, painted, resinous, or soft woods like pine. Your food will be rendered inedible, and we'd absolutely hate for that the happen.

Brother Al finishing ribs over an open flame.

Brother Al and Lyntoy getting a pork shoulder ready for the lunch rush.

OUR SECRETS*

PORK SHOULDER: Every Corky's pork shoulder is hickory smoked in our seasoned pits for 22 to 24 hours, then immediately wrapped in foil to let the natural juices flavor and moisten the meat.

*Well obviously we can't tell you all our secrets, but this is as much as Don will let us reveal!

PORK RIBS: We smoke our pork spareribs low and slow for 5 to 7 hours over hickory wood and charcoal, leaving the membrane on to help hold them together. We mop both sides with Corky's secret basting sauce, and then just before serving, we scrape off the membrane for easy eating. (For a perfectly acceptable homemade version of the basting sauce, thin a bottle of Corky's Original Barbecue Sauce with some water.) For dry ribs, we generously season the ribs with Corky's Dry Rub and finish over an open flame. For wet ribs, we follow the same process, but use a sauce mop to slather a thick coating of Corky's Original Bar-B-Q Sauce that caramelizes down into the meat, right before they come to the table. A mop holds more sauce than a brush, and you can <u>never</u> have enough sauce.

To remove or not to remove?

That, dear pit masters, is the question, and it concerns that pesky membrane on the ribs. It serves the good purpose of keeping falling-off-the-bone meat on the bones, but it's not always great to eat. So we leave it on through the entire smoking process, and just before our final rub-down or basting, we scrape the membrane off the back of the ribs to ensure Corky's signature tenderness.

19

BEEF BRISKET: Brisket is a tougher cut of beef that's tailor-made for the low, slow heat of barbecuing—7 to 9 hours over hickory and charcoal, to be exact. At Corky's we prefer to smoke our briskets in foil, allowing them to braise in their own juices, intensifying the natural flavors while keeping the meat tender and moist.

SMOKED CHICKEN: We start our "barnyard pimps" (as our cooks call them) at 7 am every morning in the smoker. Come lunch, you have succulent, moist meat that falls off the bone. We apply a nice coating of our signature chicken seasoning and smoke over hickory and charcoal for around 3 hours. We let the birds rest no less than half an hour to ensure juicy meat, before hitting the grill one last time before serving.

GRILLING TIPS:

- Hardwoods and charcoal will yield tastier fare than a gas grill. You can make easy work of building a fire with a chimney starter. This is one grilling gadget actually worth the money. Place some newspaper in the bottom, and then pour in your charcoal. Light the newspaper and let the charcoal burn until light and glowing. When it looks like this picture, it's ready for dumping into the grill box. All that said, a gas grill is better than no grill, and all the recipes in the book will work on either type. We find that the convenience of gas more than makes up for any downsides—especially for weeknight cooking.

- Always start with a clean, greased grate. A dirty grate will transfer old flavors from last weekend's cookout. It's easiest to clean with a steel brush when the grate is blazing hot.

- Salt your meat well and well in advance. By salting your meat at least an hour (and up to 24 hours) before cooking, the salt can penetrate the meat, adding flavor and helping insure a juicier end piece. Think of it like a dry version of a brine.

- Slather your sauces late in the game. Many sauces contain sugars that will quickly burn on the grill, so it's best to smear with sauces near the end of cooking instead of early on.

- Know your heat. With grill cooking, you're often left to guess the level of the heat. Follow our trusty guide for more accurate cooking.

Pitmaster Jack Holt

We pay a lot for our ribs. We're buying the absolute best quality ribs—a 2⅓ cut St. Louis rib—and having them trimmed to our exact specifications so they don't have all that excess cartilage and fat and false lean meat. This focus on quality all goes back to my dad. His theory was, "If you take an A-grade raw product, you have a chance to have an A-grade finished product. If you start with a C-grade raw, you'll never have an A-grade finished product." Those are the kinds of things that separate us from the other barbecue joints.

— Barry Pelts, co-owner

Testing Grill Temperature, Corky's-Style

Hold your hand, palm-side down, in the location where your food will be placed. Start counting one Mississippi, two Mississippi, three . . . Use the chart below to determine the heat level of your grill.

Number of seconds you can hold your hand above the grill:

2 Mississippi = High grill temperature

3 Mississippi = Medium-high grill temperature

4 Mississippi = Medium grill temperature

5 Mississippi = Medium-low grill temperature

6 Mississippi = Low grill temperature

The USDA recommendations for internal meat temperatures run slightly higher than most cooks and chefs prefer. We've included both temperatures to let you decide which is right for you.

Remove the meat at least 5 degrees cooler than your desired end temperature because meat continues cooking even off the grill. Unless you work the line in a restaurant kitchen and can accurately guess the temperature of a piece of meat with the touch of a finger, we highly recommend you invest in a digital instant read thermometer. Your taste buds will thank you, as will your dinner guests.

Let your meat rest at least a third of the time it took to grill it. When you slice meat straight off the grill, juices pour onto the cutting board. By letting it rest, the juices have the chance to redistribute completely and evenly throughout the meat and thicken slightly as it cools.

Final Internal Temperatures for Cooked Meats

MEAT	USDA	CORKY'S
Beef Rare	N/A	125°F
Beef Medium-rare	145°F	130°F
Beef Medium	160°F	135-140°F
Beef Medium-well	N/A	140-150°F
Beef Well done	170°F	155+°F
Ground beef	N/A	160°F
Pork Rare	N/A	145°F
Pork Medium	150°F	150°F
Pork Well done	160°F	160°F
Ground pork	160°F	160°F
Chicken	165°F	165°F

Fruit and Vegetable Grilling Tips

Grilling fruits and vegetables brings out their natural sweetness, enhancing the flavors when they are lightly charred. Follow these tips for optimum results:

• Cut vegetables into uniformly sized pieces so they will cook evenly.

• Soak vegetables in cold water before grilling to prevent drying out.

• Brush the vegetables with an oil-based marinade to keep them from sticking to the grill.

• Use a coarse sea salt on the outside of vegetables to draw moisture to the outer layers, keeping them from burning, and intensifying the sweet flavors of the vegetables.

• When grilling vegetables on skewers, use two parallel skewers to keep the vegetables from spinning when turning on the grill.

• Conventional wisdom says to soak wooden skewers, but tests show that they tend to burn whether soaked or not. Instead, wrap the exposed ends of the skewers in foil or set a piece of foil between the exposed ends of a row of skewers and the grate. If you do soak your skewers, use a fruit juice to add another layer of flavor. Or consider using the woody stem of rosemary as a scented skewer.

• Vegetables are done when they have browned grill marks and are tender when pierced with fork.

A Note on Sauces and Rubs

BARBECUE SAUCE: Barbecue sauce is slathered over meat at the end of the cooking process and is also served as an accompaniment to the meat after it's cooked. It's traditionally made with tomatoes, onion, mustard, garlic, and brown sugar; vinegar, beer, and wine are also popular ingredients.

DRY RUBS: Dry rubs are any mixture of dry spices and herbs used to flavor meat and vegetables. Rubs can help tenderize the meat as well as add unlimited flavor combinations. To use, evenly sprinkle the seasoning on all sides and massage into the meat well ahead of a cooking. Avoid dry rubs with too much sugar, as the sugar can cook too quickly, causing the outside of your food to burn. Add cider vinegar or fruit juice to your dry rub to transform it into a paste. See pages 28-35 in the next chapter for a wide variety of rub and sauce recipes.

Of course, if you don't want to make your own, Corky's sauces and dry rubs are available in grocery stores, at all Corky's BBQ locations, and online at CorkysBBQ.com.

Corky's meat products are available frozen in grocery stores, online at CorkysBBQ.com, and QVC.com. To serve, simply thaw, heat, and eat. You can microwave the meats, but if Don Pelts gets wind of how you're treating his ribs, we cannot be responsible for what might happen. For superior results—and a happy Don—we strongly encourage you prepare our frozen products the same way we like to cook—low and slow. The tender, fall-off-the-bone ribs and smoky, moist pulled chicken and pork shoulder will be well worth it.

SAUCES, RUBS, BREADS, & SPREADS

CONSIDER THE RECIPES IN THIS CHAPTER YOUR ⊠SECRET WEAPON. SOON ENOUGH, FOLKS WILL BE BEGGING FOR YOUR BARBEQUE SAUCE, DEMANDING - STRAWBERRY JAM IN HAND - THAT YOU PASS THEM ANOTHER STEAMY HOT BISCUIT, AND DREAMING OF ANOTHER PAT OF THAT fanciful BUTTER - THAT MAKES THE WHOLE TABLE swoon!

Apple-Cheddar Cornbread

Southern Gal Biscuits

DRY RUBS

Everybody has their own secret for the best dry rub, and we've got a bumper crop of Corky's favorites for you. You'll just have to try them all and see which one tickles your fancy. They can be stored in an airtight container in a cool, dry place for up to six months. As with all dried herbs and spices, their flavors will begin to lessen with time. Before using your dry rub in a recipe or on meats, be sure to remix thoroughly with a good shake.

CORKY'S HOUSE RUB

This spice mix is as close as you're ever going to get to the real thing, Corky's famous dry rub. It's not exact, but it's still great—put it on meats well ahead of smoking or grilling for optimum flavor.

 YIELDS: scant ½ cup

2 tablespoons plus 2 teaspoons paprika

4 teaspoons dried oregano

2 teaspoons garlic powder

2 teaspoons freshly ground black pepper

2 teaspoons salt

Accent Flavor Enhancer *(to taste)*

Mix all the ingredients together in a small bowl and store in an airtight container. Use as a substitute for Corky's Bar-B-Q Dry Rub if the real version isn't handy.

BIG JACK'S KC-STYLE DRY RUB

YIELDS: 1¼ cups

½ cup paprika

¼ cup garlic powder

¼ cup mild chili powder

3 tablespoons freshly ground black pepper

2 tablespoons onion powder

1 tablespoon brown sugar

1 tablespoon ground cumin

2 teaspoons dry mustard

Mix all the ingredients together in a small bowl and store in an airtight container.

BROTHER LLOYD'S DRY RUB

YIELDS: 1 cup

¼ cup paprika

2 tablespoons salt

2 tablespoons sugar

2 tablespoons brown sugar

2 tablespoons ground cumin

2 tablespoons chili powder

2 tablespoons freshly ground black pepper

1 tablespoon cayenne pepper

Mix all the ingredients in a small bowl and store in an airtight container.

Chief pitmaster Robert Moye is one of the most recognized and loved Corky's family members. Although he has now relinquished the Corky's Bar-B-Q pits to his protégés in exchange for a more relaxed lifestyle of backyard Bar-B-Qs, he is often seen at events or visiting the Memphis stores— just making sure everyone is keeping up to his standards.

PITMASTER MOYE'S RIB & TENDERLOIN DRY RUB

 YIELDS: ½ cup

3 tablespoons brown sugar

2 tablespoons paprika

1½ tablespoons salt

1½ tablespoons freshly ground black pepper

1 teaspoon garlic powder

Mix all the ingredients together in a small bowl and store in an airtight container.

Chief Pitmaster Robert Moye

KICK-UP-THE-HEAT DRY RUB

 YIELDS: 1½ cups

1 cup chili powder

¼ cup garlic salt

2 tablespoons freshly ground black pepper

1 tablespoon cayenne pepper

1 tablespoon brown sugar

1 tablespoon ground white pepper

Mix all the ingredients in a small bowl and store in an airtight container.

JOE LEE'S KANSAS CITY-STYLE DRY RUB

 YIELDS: 1 cup

⅓ cup sugar

¼ cup paprika

1 tablespoon freshly ground black pepper

1 tablespoon salt

1 tablespoon chili powder

1 tablespoon garlic powder

1 tablespoon onion powder

1 teaspoon cayenne pepper

Mix all the ingredients in a small bowl and store in an airtight container.

O'DILLON'S DRY RUB

YIELDS: 1 cup
CORKY'S FRIEND: Jim O'Dillon

¼ cup sea salt

¼ cup lightly packed dark brown sugar

¼ cup paprika

3 tablespoons ground black pepper

1 tablespoon garlic powder

1 teaspoon dried onion flakes

1 teaspoon cayenne pepper

1 teaspoon ground allspice

Mix all the ingredients in a small bowl and store in an airtight container. Season meat at least two hours prior to cooking.

JIM'S ZESTY BAR-B-Q SAUCE

YIELDS: 2 cups
CORKY'S FRIEND: Jim O'Dillon

1¾ cups ketchup

1½ cups lightly packed dark brown sugar

2 tablespoons Worcestershire sauce

1 tablespoon molasses

1 tablespoon apple cider vinegar

1 tablespoon sugar

½ teaspoon freshly ground black pepper

½ teaspoon ground cinnamon

½ teaspoon liquid smoke

⅛ teaspoon ground cloves

⅛ teaspoon ground orange zest

Mix all the ingredients thoroughly in a stainless steel saucepan and bring to a simmer. Reduce the heat to the lowest setting possible to maintain a simmer and simmer to allow flavors to meld, about 1 hour.

NORTH CAROLINA VINEGAR SAUCE

YIELDS: 3 cups
CORKY'S FAMILY: Tom Keyes

2 cups cider vinegar

⅔ cup ketchup

2 tablespoons brown sugar

2 teaspoons kosher salt

2 teaspoons Worcestershire sauce

1 teaspoon crushed red pepper flakes

In a medium saucepan over medium heat, combine all the ingredients. Bring to a simmer, stirring often, and cook until the sugar and salt have dissolved, about 3 minutes. Remove from the heat and serve, or cool and store in an airtight container in the refrigerator for up to one week.

STRAWBERRY JALAPENO BAR-B-Q SAUCE

This spicy sauce is great with Lil' Smokies, meatballs, and as a dip for fried catfish.

YIELDS: 4½ cups
CORKY'S FRIEND: Connie Crabtree-Burritt

1 (16-ounce) package frozen strawberries

2 cups Corky's Original Recipe Bar-B-Q sauce

1 cup ketchup

1 tablespoon hot sauce *(Tiger sauce preferred)*

1 large garlic clove, minced

½ teaspoon freshly ground black pepper

1 medium jalapeño pepper, seeded and chopped

Purée the strawberries in a food processor. Transfer the strawberry purée to a saucepan; add the remaining ingredients and bring to a simmer over medium heat. Simmer until heated through and reduced slightly, about 4 to 5 minutes. Use immediately or cover and store in the refrigerator up to three days.

BAR-B-Q RANCH DIPPING SAUCE AND DRESSING

Corky's serves this with their onion loaf and barbecue salad. It makes a great dipping sauce for everything from chicken nuggets to fried pickles.

YIELDS: 2 servings

1 cup Corky's Original Recipe Bar-B-Q Sauce

1 cup ranch dressing

Whisk the Bar-B-Q sauce and ranch dressing in a medium bowl to blend. Cover and store in the refrigerator until ready to use.

the bomb-diggity. My booty is two inches thicker because of this place it was so good. I ate there almost every day I was in Memphis. I had the turkey ribs, and brisket (during multiple trips) and I loved the twice-baked potato salad. (It's the best potato salad I have ever had.) The sweet tea was also fabulous. There are few places that I dream of going back to, and this is one of them—I can't wait. Yum-O!

— *a review from Kara, East Point, GA*

CHIPOTLE MAYONNAISE

This Chipotle Mayonnaise enhances the flavors of just about everything it touches. Try it with grilled okra or okra fritters, and with potato chips or French fries. Add it to grilled pork tenderloin sandwiches or hamburgers, or use it as a dipping sauce for chicken strips or fried catfish. We haven't found anything that it doesn't work well with.

YIELDS: 1½ cups

CORKY'S FAMILY: Sheila Thomas

1 cup mayonnaise

2 tablespoons finely chopped chives

½ lime, juiced

2 garlic cloves, minced

2 canned chipotle peppers in adobo sauce

1½ teaspoons adobo sauce *(plus additional to taste)*

Salt and freshly ground black pepper *(to taste)*

Combine all the ingredients except the salt and pepper in a food processor and process until smooth. Taste and season with additional adobo sauce, salt, and pepper as needed. (Keep in mind that the flavors will develop and it will taste a bit spicier after a few hours.) Cover and refrigerate for up to one week.

ROB'S CARIBBEAN MUSTARD BAR-B-Q SAUCE

This Caribbean-style curried fruit hot sauce is a universal crowd-pleaser. This recipe can easily be halved and it goes with everything—pork, beef, fish, or chicken. You can transform this sauce into a tropical salad dressing by diluting it with water and additional vinegar.

YIELDS: 5 cups

CORKY'S FRIEND: Rob Cosgrove

1½ cups (12 ounces) yellow mustard

¾ cup sliced fresh papaya

¾ cup (6 ounces) pineapple juice

¾ cup extra-virgin olive oil

¾ cup white vinegar

¼ cup lightly packed brown sugar

¼ cup orange juice

¼ cup honey

¼ cup molasses

1 tablespoon chili powder

1 tablespoon ground cumin

1 tablespoon ground turmeric

1 tablespoon ground allspice

1 tablespoon curry powder

Salt and freshly ground black pepper *(to taste)*

Canned chipotle peppers in adobo sauce *(to taste)*

Place all the ingredients except the salt, pepper, and chipotle in a blender; blend on high. Season to taste with the salt and pepper. Add the chipotle peppers in adobo sauce, half a pepper at a time, blending and tasting between additions until the desired heat is reached. (For an even spicier sauce, substitute Scotch bonnet peppers for the chipotle.) Use immediately or cover and refrigerate for up to two weeks.

GARY'S SPICY BRISKET GRAVY

"Don't limit yourself to brisket for this gravy," says recipe contributor and Texan Gary Carter. "This regional favorite from North Texas makes a great dunking sauce for some of those fine Corky's ribs that are shipped to pork-less areas here in the Lone Star State." The gravy also is delicious served atop Southern Gal Biscuits (page 38).

YIELDS: 4 cups

CORKY'S FRIEND: Gary Carter

1 quart drippings from smoked brisket

½ cup all-purpose flour

½ cup warm water

2 tablespoons cider vinegar

1 tablespoon unsalted butter

1 tablespoon cayenne pepper

1 tablespoon Worcestershire sauce

1 garlic clove, crushed

1 teaspoon ketchup

1 teaspoon mustard

1 teaspoon salt

1 teaspoon freshly ground black pepper

Bring the smoked brisket drippings to a simmer in a heavy-bottomed pot over medium heat. Add all the other ingredients and whisk briskly while simmering until thickened slightly.

Corky's has the best ribs in the country, and the most addictive dry rub I've ever tasted!

— *Gary Carter*

MOM'S TOMATO GRAVY

"After my mother passed away, I realized that this tomato gravy was the only recipe she had written down. I have offered country cooking to my now decidedly Midwestern family with varying success, but this gravy always satisfies," says Eric. "I'm thrilled to have an opportunity to share this treasured dish with others. Apparently bacon and tomatoes have a successful history together; the combination works on just about anything—biscuits, eggs, fricasseed chicken, or country-fried steak. The bacon is the key starter for the flavor, so don't skimp."

YIELDS: 3 cups

CORKY'S FRIEND: Eric Wright

6 strips bacon

¼ cup finely chopped onion

⅓ cup all-purpose flour

1 (28-ounce) can Italian stewed tomatoes

⅓ cup milk *(if needed)*

1 teaspoon Italian seasoning

Salt and freshly ground black pepper *(to taste)*

Cook the bacon over medium heat in skillet to render the fat. Remove the bacon and reserve for another use. (Or eat!) Add the onion to bacon drippings and sauté until tender, about 5 to 6 minutes. Reduce the heat to low and slowly add the flour to the bacon fat, whisking constantly until you have a paste the consistency of pancake batter. Cook for 3 minutes, stirring occasionally. Add the tomatoes and bring to a simmer; stir until thick. If the gravy is too thick, thin it with a little milk. Stir in the Italian seasoning, then season to taste with salt and pepper. Serve with the Southern Gal Biscuits on page 38.

I live in the Midwest, but my family is from Lebanon, Tennessee. While visiting relatives in the area a few years ago, we happened into a Corky's during our tour of Memphis. We were hooked from bite one. We regularly order Corky's sauce and rub by mail now and plan on visiting again next summer.

— Eric Wright

SOUTHERN GAL BISCUITS

We tested scores of biscuit recipes, but this one rose above the rest. Literally. Hot biscuits with butter, jam, honey, or gravy—any way you top them will bring a smile to your face.

For cheese biscuits, stir in 1 cup shredded Cheddar cheese before adding the buttermilk. Drop by rounded tablespoonfuls into a greased cake pan, and bake as directed below. After baking them, combine ¼ cup (½ stick) melted butter with ¼ teaspoon garlic powder, and brush over the warm biscuits.

YIELDS: 8 to 12 biscuits

CORKY'S FAMILY: Dona Watts

Nonstick cooking spray, oil, or butter

1½ cups self-rising flour *(White Lily preferred)*

1 tablespoon sugar

¼ teaspoon salt

¼ cup vegetable shortening, chilled

1¼ cups buttermilk

1 cup all-purpose flour

2 tablespoons (¼ stick) butter, melted

Preheat the oven to 450°F. Using nonstick spray, oil, or butter, grease a round cake pan. Combine the self-rising flour, sugar, and salt in a large bowl. Cut in the shortening with a pastry blender or fork until pea-size crumbs form. Stir in the buttermilk with a fork. (The dough will be very wet and will resemble cottage cheese.)

Pour the all-purpose flour into a shallow bowl. With a tablespoon or ice cream scoop, scoop a lump of the dough into the flour; lightly coat the dough on the outside to prevent sticking. With floured hands, shape the dough into a ball, shake off the excess flour, and place in the prepared pan. The biscuits should touch each other to help them rise instead of spreading. (Who wants a flat biscuit?) Bake in the center of the oven until golden brown, about 18 to 20 minutes. Brush the biscuits with melted butter and serve hot.

Southern Gal Biscuits with Mom's Tomato Gravy

APPLE-CHEDDAR CORN BREAD

These cornbread wedges embody the flavors of autumn. The apples lend moistness to the cornmeal, and Cheddar is a classic partner to this fruit.

YIELDS: 8 servings

CORKY'S FAMILY: Sheila Thomas

Nonstick cooking spray, oil, or butter

1 cup cornmeal

1 cup all-purpose flour

½ cup sugar

1 tablespoon baking powder

1 cup milk

¼ cup (½ stick) butter, melted

1 large egg

2 small tart red apples, peeled and chopped

½ cup (2 ounces) shredded Cheddar cheese

Preheat the oven to 425°F. Using the nonstick spray, oil, or butter, grease a 9-inch round baking pan or iron skillet. Combine the cornmeal, flour, sugar, and baking powder in a large bowl, whisking to mix well. Using an electric mixer with a large bowl, beat the milk, butter, and egg at medium speed until well blended. Add the flour mixture and stir just until moistened. Fold in the apples and cheese, and pour the mixture into the prepared pan. Bake until a toothpick inserted in the center comes out clean, about 20 to 25 minutes. Cool in the pan on a wire rack.

As a former pig-lover/eater, I was fortunate enough to try this place during my grand tour of the South last year. Growing up, I had always heard about Corky's. My dad's friend would give us BBQ sauce from Corky's, and I always found it amazing. My friend tried the dry ribs while I tried the wet ones. We couldn't figure out which we liked best— they're all amazing!! The meat is so tender and easily slides of the ribs. The cole slaw, hush puppies, potato salad, onion blossom—everything was amazing!! If I ever find myself in Tennessee, I will definitely make a stop at Corky's and break my no-pork vow because it's too much awesomeness to pass up!

— a review from Guava, San Francisco

SWEET POTATO BISCUITS

This recipe comes from Holly Clegg, one of our favorite cookbook authors with a penchant for all things sweet potato or yam. Holly often serves pulled pork over these biscuits as an open-face brunch sandwich. These biscuits are even better prepared with fresh Louisiana yams—peeled, boiled, drained, and mashed—instead of the canned variety. If using fresh yams, increase the milk to 1 cup and omit the syrup.

YIELDS: 18 biscuits

CORKY'S FRIEND: Holly Clegg

4 cups all-purpose baking mix (such as Bisquick)

1 (15-ounce) can sweet potatoes or yams in syrup, drained (reserve ½ cup syrup) and mashed

½ cup milk

All-purpose flour *(for rolling biscuits)*

Preheat the oven to 450°F. In a large bowl, combine the baking mix, mashed sweet potatoes, reserved ½ cup syrup, and milk. Mix well. Turn the dough out onto a floured surface and roll or pat out to 1-inch thickness. Use a 2-inch round cookie cutter or glass to cut out the biscuits, being careful not to twist the cutter. Place the dough rounds on a baking sheet and bake until golden brown, about 10 to 12 minutes.

> My husband's father had a chain of retail stores, so he understood what it meant to work in a family business. My dad and brother are overflowing with ideas. My husband, Andy, takes the big ideas and makes everyone look at the details. They all balance each other perfectly.
>
> — *Tricia Woodman, daughter of Corky's founder*

WOMEN'S EXCHANGE PIMENTO CHEESE

Pimento cheese is the peanut butter of the South, with as many variations as Texas has for salsa. This particular rendition has a loyal following at the Women's Exchange Tea Room, a Memphis landmark. Why are we so enamored with this simple cheese spread? Well, what's not to love? It's easy to make, it's cheap, and it tastes great. It doesn't make soft white bread go soggy, and it keeps well. It's good between two slices of bread, lining a rib of celery, packed into a cherry tomato, or perched on a cracker. It's heaven on a hamburger or a hot dog, or eaten with a spoon right out of the crock. Substitute Colby cheese or Monterey Jack cheese for any one of the cheeses listed if desired.

YIELDS: 3 cups

1½ cups (6 ounces) grated Parmesan cheese

1 cup (4 ounces) shredded Cheddar cheese

1 cup (4 ounces) shredded smoked Gouda cheese

1 (7-ounce) jar diced pimentos, drained

1 cup mayonnaise

1 jalapeño pepper, seeded and minced

1 tablespoon vinegar

1 teaspoon salt

1 teaspoon freshly ground black pepper

Cayenne pepper *(to taste)*

Combine the cheeses and pimentos in a large bowl and mix well. In a medium bowl, combine the mayonnaise, jalapeño, vinegar, salt, and black pepper; season to taste with cayenne pepper. Stir the mayonnaise mixture into the cheese mixture. Cover and refrigerate until ready to use (up to two weeks). Use as a sandwich filling, a spread for crackers, or as a dip.

I don't know what else to say other than Corky's has, hands down, the best ribs I've _ever_ had.

Before I go into the details, let me give a quick back-story: My wife and I decided to take a BBQ trip through KC, Texas, and back through Memphis. We hit several well-known spots and some holes in the wall.

We had the best sauce we've ever had in KC, the best brisket in TX, but the best overall BBQ place we hit on our last night of the trip before we headed home. Honestly, I didn't expect anything special. Man, was I wrong.

We pulled into Corky's about 8:45 p.m. and were expecting the place to be somewhat empty, being that late on a weeknight. Nope—there was a line out the door. I walked up to ask how long the wait was and the hostess said we could sit at the bar right away if we wanted—food was the same. Done.

My wife ordered the pulled pork and I ordered the dry rub ribs. I don't recall what we even got as sides other than they brought out these warm rolls that were beyond awesome. Not sure what they packed in there to make them so delicious. Anyway, we were chatting with the bartender who was a blast and made us feel like we were regulars.

The food came out in a timely fashion and what transpired next forever changed my life. I grabbed for one of the dry rubbed ribs and as it pulled away from its siblings on my plate,

the aroma of smokey flavor hit my nose. As I bit into the tender meat, the dry rub and smoke flavor and succulent goodness of the rib all swirled together to form a cornucopia of delight that tickled my taste buds and sent me into gastronomy ecstasy. I had to have my wife pinch me just to remind me that I wasn't dreaming. I couldn't believe what I just ate.

Now, my wife hates ribs to the point that the look of them grosses her out. But she could see the look of bliss on my face and knew something was up. I told her that I know she hates ribs but she HAD to try this.

It was unlike anything you've ever had. Reluctantly she took a small nibble and was instantly won over. I could see the doubt melt away and she was hooked. She couldn't believe it either and asked if we could split our meals! Thirty seconds earlier she was a hater of ribs, but that one bite literally transformed her life.

We are planning a weekend trip to Memphis just to go to Corky's. I can't wait!

— a review from John, Aurora, IL

STEAK BUTTER

YIELDS: 8 servings
CORKY'S FAMILY: Jimmy Stovall

½ cup (1 stick) butter, softened

1 tablespoon Dijon mustard

1 garlic clove, minced

Chopped green onions
(to taste)

Stir the butter, mustard, and garlic together in a small bowl; stir in enough of the chopped green onions to taste. Line a work surface with a piece of parchment paper or plastic wrap. Scrape the butter mixture into a line about 5 inches long on the paper or plastic wrap and form it into a log, rolling up to enclose and twisting the ends to seal. Refrigerate until hardened, at least 30 minutes. As you pull steaks or chops off of the grill, add a slice or a scoop of the steak butter to the top and let it slowly melt while the steak is resting.

HARRIET'S HOTEL BUTTER

Carol Sweeney, a longtime Corky's employee, got this recipe from her grandmother Harriet Keyes, who developed it after she enjoyed a particularly delightful meal at a swanky hotel. The meal came with an equally swanky butter, and so Harriet decided to recreate it for her own guests at home.

YIELDS: 8 servings
CORKY'S FAMILY: Carol Sweeney

½ cup (1 stick) unsalted butter, softened

2 tablespoons minced flat-leaf parsley

1 tablespoon freshly squeezed lemon juice

¼ teaspoon sea salt

Stir all the ingredients together in a small bowl. Line a work surface with a piece of parchment paper or plastic wrap. Scrape the butter mixture into a line about 5 inches long on the paper or plastic wrap and form it into a log, rolling up to enclose and twisting the ends to seal. Refrigerate until hardened, at least 30 minutes. Slice into round disks for serving.

Fruit Tea

Corky's Popcorn

Smoked Sausage and Cheese Tray with Spicy Mustard Dip

STARTERS & DRINKS

WE LOVE **ALL** THE RECIPES IN THIS BOOK BUT LETS BE **HONEST**: YOU COULD THROW A PARTY FROM THIS CHAPTER ALONE. THINK **CORKY'S** FAMOUS BBQ NACHOS, SOME PECAN -CRUSTED SPINACH -ARTICHOKE DIP, CAROL SWEENEY'S IN-DEMAND PORK MUFFINS, AND **SMOKY** SWEET * CHICKEN BACON BITES, ALL WASHED DOWN WITH SULTRY SUMMER PEACH TEA. OR OLD-FASHIONED LEMONADE. OR A SPIKED VERSION OF **BOTH**!

MEMPHIS BAR-B-Q NACHOS

This riff on classic nachos is Memphis through and through. You'll find it at sports bars around town, at home on Friday nights, and at Corky's every day of the year.

YIELDS: 8 to 10 servings

CORKY'S FAMILY: Steve Brown

1 pound Corky's Bar-B-Q Pulled Pork or Chicken

1 (16-ounce) container refrigerated cheese dip

1 (1-pound) bag round corn tortilla chips

1 (18-ounce) bottle Corky's Original Recipe Bar-B-Q Sauce

1 cup shredded iceberg lettuce

½ cup chopped green onions

1 large tomato, chopped

¼ cup (about) sliced fresh or canned jalapeño slices

Corky's Bar-B-Q Dry Rub *(to taste)*

Preheat the oven to 350°F. Place the meat in a casserole dish, cover with foil to keep it from drying out, and set in the oven until warmed through, about 35 minutes. In a microwave-safe bowl, microwave the cheese dip until melted.

Empty the tortilla chips onto a large platter, spreading them evenly out to the edges. Layer the warm meat, cheese dip, Bar-B-Q sauce, lettuce, green onions, and tomatoes over the chips. Add enough jalapeño slices to suit your taste, and finish with a light sprinkling of dry rub. Serve immediately and watch them disappear!

My favorite thing from Corky's? The nachos. Obviously. I'd never in my life heard of putting pulled pork on nachos. The head buyer and I went to Memphis to try Corky's in person. Jimmy and Barry ordered the whole menu, I think—you name it, we had it. I was blown away by the nachos. Every time Jimmy shows them on the air at QVC, I sneak into the prep kitchen to get my fix. (I don't think he knows that.)

— *Lauren Baker, QVC*

PORK MUFFINS

"Back in 1988, a friend of mine who was going off to college knew that I was looking for a job," says Carol. "She insisted I go and meet with Robbie, the Queen Bee of Corky's. At that time, you had to meet with Robbie before you could even fill out an application. Luckily, she hired me on the spot. I have worked every position in the restaurant and at four different Corky's locations. My sisters and brothers have also worked at Corky's throughout the years. My kids have Corky's in their blood and cannot wait to be old enough to work there!"

Be sure to grease your muffin pans well so these muffins will release easily, or use cupcake liners to make even easier work of it.

YIELDS: 12 muffins

CORKY'S FAMILY: Carol Sweeney

Nonstick cooking spray, oil, or butter

4 tablespoons (½ stick) unsalted butter, melted *(no substitutions)*

1½ cups all-purpose flour

2½ teaspoons baking powder

1 cup sugar

¾ cup milk

1 large egg

¼ teaspoon vanilla extract

1 cup shredded Cheddar cheese

½ pound Corky's Bar-B-Q Pork Shoulder, finely chopped

1 (18-ounce) bottle Corky's Original Recipe Bar-B-Q Sauce

Preheat the oven to 400°F. Grease a muffin pan well using cooking spray, oil, or butter. To make the batter, combine the melted butter, flour, baking powder, sugar, milk, egg, and vanilla in a large bowl. Fold in the cheese. In a separate bowl, combine the pork shoulder with enough Bar-B-Q sauce to coat the meat well.

Using a prepared muffin pan, place a teaspoonful of batter in the bottom of each cup. Follow with a tablespoonful of the meat mixture, and then cover with 2 teaspoons of batter. Repeat until all of the muffin cups are full. Bake for 20 minutes. Allow to cool slightly before removing the muffins from the pan.

CHRISTA'S STARS OF PORK

Christa has been with Corky's since 1998. This recipe has been a family favorite since Christa was in the first grade, way before she became the "Star of Pork."

YIELDS: 12 servings

CORKY'S FAMILY: Christa Gilliland

1 tablespoon vegetable oil

1 medium-size yellow bell pepper, seeded and diced

1 medium-size orange bell pepper, seeded and diced

8 ounces black olives, chopped

1 pound Corky's Bar-B-Q Pork Shoulder, finely chopped

2 (8-ounce) packages shredded Cheddar and Monterey Jack cheese mix

Nonstick cooking spray

1 (16-ounce) bottle ranch dressing

1 (12-ounce) package wonton wrappers

Corky's Bar-B-Q Dry Rub *(to taste)*

Preheat the oven to 350°F. Pour the oil into a large skillet set over medium heat. Add the peppers and olives and cook until they begin to soften, about 5 minutes. Add the pork and continue cooking until the pork is warmed through. Add the cheese and stir until it melts. Remove from heat.

Spray a muffin pan with nonstick cooking spray. Lay one wonton wrapper over each cup of the muffin pan and then lay another wonton wrapper on top, but set slightly offset to form a star pattern. Place one tablespoon of the meat and cheese mixture in the center and gently push down into the muffin cup. Repeat until all of the muffin cups are full.

Bake until the edges of the wonton are browned and slightly crispy, about 20 minutes. Remove from the oven and season to taste with dry rub. Let cool and enjoy.

CHOCOLATE-COVERED BACON

Don't knock it 'til you've tried it! Chocolate-covered bacon makes for an easy, different, and tasty presentation.

YIELDS: 18 servings

CORKY'S FAMILY: Mary Ryan

18 slices applewood-smoked bacon

2 cups semisweet chocolate chips

2 cups white chocolate chips

Arrange the bacon strips in a single layer on a foil-lined baking sheet. Place in the oven, and then set the temperature to 400°F. When the oven is preheated, your bacon is ready! Remove the bacon from the oven and drain on paper towels.

Transfer the bacon to waxed paper, leaving space between the strips.

In separate microwave-safe bowls, melt the white chocolate and the milk chocolate chips. (Microwave in 30-second increments, stirring each time, to keep from scorching.) Spoon the melted chocolate into separate pastry bags. (You can also use a resealable plastic bag and snip the corner.) Drizzle the chocolate over the bacon in a zig-zag pattern, first dark chocolate, then white, allowing the chocolate to harden between layers. Refrigerate if necessary.

CHARLENE'S CHEDDAR BACON BAR-B-Q BRUSCHETTA

These two-bite hot and cheesy appetizers can be assembled ahead of time and popped in the oven just before your guests arrive. They come courtesy of Charlene, who began her career with Corky's in 1990 at the Jackson, Tennessee, location. She then spent 9 years in New Orleans before transferring to Memphis, where she met and married Joel. They are just one of many married couples that met and still work at Corky's.

YIELDS: 16 servings

CORKY'S FAMILY: Charlene Storck

½ pound Corky's Bar-B-Q Pork Shoulder, chopped

8 slices bacon, cooked and crumbled

1 medium tomato, chopped

2 baguettes, cut into ½-inch slices

2 tablespoons olive oil

2 cups shredded Cheddar cheese

Corky's Original Recipe Bar-B-Q Sauce *(for serving)*

Preheat the broiler. In a medium bowl, mix together the pork, bacon, and tomato. Lay out the baguette slices on a sheet pan and drizzle with olive oil. Spoon the pork mixture onto the baguette slices and top with Cheddar cheese. Broil until cheese melts, about 5 minutes. Remove from the oven and drizzle with Bar-B-Q sauce. Serve immediately.

BACON BLUE CHEESE BREAD

YIELDS: 12 servings

CORKY'S FRIEND: Julie Wright

½ cup (1 stick) unsalted butter, softened

4 ounces blue cheese, crumbled, at room temperature

6 slices thick-cut bacon, cooked and crumbled

1 loaf French bread

Preheat the broiler. In a medium bowl, combine the butter, blue cheese, and bacon. Cut the bread into ⅓-inch-thick slices. Arrange the bread slices on a baking sheet in a single layer; toast under the broiler on one side only, watching carefully. Remove from the oven and spread the cheese mixture on the untoasted side of the bread. Return to the oven and broil until hot and bubbly, about 1 to 2 minutes. Serve hot.

PORK PALACE POCKETS

A family favorite – kids especially love filling the dough and crimping the sides on those homemade hot pockets. Corky's employees refer to Corky's as The Pork Palace.

Jimmy and Jill Bauer at QVC.

YIELDS: 4 servings

CORKY'S FAMILY: Carol Sweeney

½ pound Corky's Bar-B-Q Pork Shoulder, finely chopped

1 (18-ounce) bottle Corky's Original Recipe Bar-B-Q Sauce *(to taste)*

1 (8-ounce) can refrigerated crescent rolls

Preheat the oven to 375°F. In a medium bowl, mix together the pork and enough of the Bar-B-Q sauce to moisten the pork. Open the can of crescent rolls and lay out the dough in 4 rectangles. Press the perforations to seal. Place some of the pork mixture onto half of the rectangle, and then fold the remaining dough over. Press the edges with a fork to crimp and seal. Place the pockets on a cookie sheet and bake until lightly browned, about 10 to 12 minutes. Serve with additional Bar-B-Q sauce on the side for dipping.

CLASSIC DEVILED EGGS

YIELDS: 12 servings

CORKY'S FAMILY: Jan Klein

12 large eggs, hard-boiled and peeled

¼ cup mayonnaise

2 tablespoons yellow mustard

2 tablespoons sweet relish

Salt and freshly ground pepper *(to taste)*

Corky's Bar-B-Q Dry Rub *(to taste)*

Slice the hard-boiled eggs in half lengthwise, placing the yolks in a large bowl and arranging the whites on a platter. Mash the yolks with a fork. Add the mayonnaise, mustard, and relish to the yolks and thoroughly combine. Season to taste with salt and pepper. Spoon or pipe the filling into the egg halves and garnish with the dry rub. Chill before serving.

BAR-B-Q DEVILED EGGS

No potluck is complete without the requisite deviled eggs. This version lets the creamy, eggy goodness shine through, with a hint of barbecue sauce in the mix and a sprinkling of barbecue dry rub in lieu of the typical paprika. It's a delicious twist on the classic. Jimmy Stovall alone ate almost a dozen at the photo shoot!

YIELDS: 8 servings

CORKY'S FAMILY: Elliott Ann

8 large eggs, hard-boiled and peeled

2 tablespoons mayonnaise

1 tablespoon Corky's Original Recipe Bar-B-Q Sauce

1 teaspoon mustard

Corky's Bar-B-Q Dry Rub *(to taste)*

Slice the hard-boiled eggs in half lengthwise, putting the yolks into a medium bowl and arranging the whites on a platter. Mash the yolks with a fork and mix in the mayonnaise, Bar-B-Q sauce, and mustard. Spoon the yolk mixture into a sturdy, resealable bag, push the contents to one corner, and snip off the corner, making a pastry bag. Pipe the yolk mixture into the whites. Sprinkle with dry rub and serve.

THE PERFECT BOIL

For perfect hard-boiled eggs, start by placing the eggs in a pot and filling it with cold water until the eggs are covered by about an inch. Salt the water, set the pot over high heat, and bring to a boil. Keep an eye on the pot: As soon as the water comes to a rolling boil, remove from the burner, and cover. Let the eggs stand for 15 minutes. This process ensures that the eggs cook all the way through but do not become overcooked, which is what causes the yolks to turn greenish-gray.

After they stand for 15 minutes, remove the lid and place the eggs under cold running water. Once the eggs reach a lukewarm temperature, place them in the refrigerator until completely cool, about two hours. Cooling your eggs will make them easier to peel, because the cooked egg separates from the shell. Crack and peel your eggs, starting from the wider portion of the egg.

LEW'S FRIED DILL PICKLES

The Hollywood Cafe in Robinsonville, Mississippi, made fried dill pickles famous with their Memphis guests. We carry on the Southern tradition here with a Corkified version from one of our managers, Lew Bilbrey. He's been with Corky's for 15 years. When we get a wild hair to add a new menu item, Lew is our go-to guy for developing and tweaking the recipe until it is just right. Try these fried dill pickles with the Bar-B-Q Ranch (page 33) or the Strawberry Jalapeño Bar-B-Q Sauce (page 33).

YIELDS: 8 servings

CORKY'S FAMILY: Lew Bilbrey

1 cup all-purpose flour

¼ cup cornstarch

1 teaspoon baking powder

¼ teaspoon salt

1 tablespoon Corky's Bar-B-Q Dry Rub

1 cup ice water

1 medium egg yolk

2 tablespoons dill pickle juice

Vegetable oil *(for frying)*

4 cups drained dill pickle slices

In a large bowl, combine the flour, cornstarch, baking powder, salt, and dry rub. Make a well in the center and add the water, egg yolk, and pickle juice. Whisk the batter together until smooth. Cover and refrigerate for 30 minutes.

In a large pot, Dutch oven, or electric fryer, heat at least 2 inches of oil to 375°F. In batches, dip pickle slices in the batter, coating them lightly and evenly. Carefully place the coated slices in the hot oil, taking care not to overcrowd the pan. Fry until golden and crisp, 1½ to 2 minutes. Drain on paper towels and serve immediately.

BLUE CHEESE ASPARAGUS WRAPS

You can certainly use canned asparagus, but why miss the splendor of spring? Choose fresh asparagus instead for a brighter green, crisper finish. Substitute a herbed cheese like Boursin if you're not fond of blue.

YIELDS: 36 servings

CORKY'S FRIEND: Harriet Keyes

4 ounces blue cheese

1 (8-ounce) package cream cheese, softened

1 large egg, lightly beaten

2 loaves whole wheat bread, sliced very thinly

2 (14.5-ounce) cans whole asparagus spears or 1 large bunch fresh asparagus, blanched

1 cup (2 sticks) unsalted butter, melted

½ cup grated Parmesan cheese *(about 2 ounces)*

Corky's Bar-B-Q Dry Rub *(for sprinkling)*

To make the spread, mix together the blue cheese, cream cheese, and egg in a medium bowl.

Preheat the oven to 350°F. Cut the crusts off the bread slices and roll each piece flat with a rolling pin. Spread the cheese mixture onto one side of each slice, follow with 1 asparagus spear, and roll up to enclose asparagus. Brush melted butter on the outside of each roll and sprinkle with Parmesan cheese. Slice each roll into 3 pieces, and place on a baking sheet. (For best results, freeze before baking.) Bake for 20 minutes, and then sprinkle with dry rub before serving.

SMOKED SAUSAGE AND CHEESE TRAY WITH SPICY MUSTARD DIP

YIELDS: 12 servings

CORKY'S FRIEND: Julie Wright

½ cup dry mustard

½ cup white vinegar

1 large egg, beaten

1 cup sugar

3 pounds fully-cooked smoked sausages

Corky's Bar-B-Q Dry Rub *(to taste)*

8 ounces Cheddar cheese, sliced or cubed

8 ounces pepper jack cheese, sliced or cubed

8 ounces Swiss cheese, sliced or cubed

12 pickle spears

12 pepperoncini peppers

Crackers *(for serving)*

To make the mustard dip, combine the dry mustard and vinegar in a medium size bowl. Let stand for three hours, stirring occasionally. Add the egg and sugar to the mixture and stir to combine. Transfer to a medium saucepan and cook over low heat, stirring frequently, until the mixture thickens. Remove from the heat and allow to cool.

To heat the smoked sausages, prepare a grill for low-heat cooking. Grill the sausages for 4 to 5 minutes on each side, and then drain on paper towels. Cut the grilled sausages into bite-size pieces and sprinkle with dry rub.

Arrange the cheeses, pickles, and pepperoncini peppers on a serving plate and sprinkle lightly with dry rub. Add the smoked sausages and serve them along with the mustard sauce and your favorite crackers.

PEPPERONI SPINACH BITES

These pepperoni bites are the first thing to disappear from any of our party spreads. Use seasoned feta cheese for an extra layer of flavor. They're best served piping hot, but can be assembled ahead and stored in the refrigerator. Throw them in the oven just before your guests arrive.

YIELDS: 12 servings

CORKY'S FRIEND: Mary Roberts

Nonstick cooking spray

1 (8-ounce) package pepperoni slices

1 (10-ounce) package frozen spinach, thawed, water squeezed out

1 (8-ounce) package cream cheese, softened

1 (8-ounce) package feta cheese, crumbled

1 tablespoon minced garlic

2 cups shredded mozzarella cheese

Preheat the oven to 375°F. Spray a mini muffin pan with cooking spray and place a pepperoni slice in the bottom of each cup. Mix all the other ingredients together in a large bowl. Place a spoonful of the mixture on top of each slice of pepperoni. Bake until the filling bubbles and cheese melts, about 15 minutes. Allow the bites to cool for a few minutes so they are easier to remove from the pan, and then serve warm.

Corky's is a staple to this community because everybody knows the Pelts family. They give back to the community. I'm very proud to be affiliated with them.

— Donna Thorsen, *Corky's employee for more than 15 years*

SMOKY SWEET CHICKEN BACON BITES

YIELDS: 12 servings

CORKY'S FRIEND: Mary Roberts

1¼ pounds chicken tenders

1 cup lightly packed brown sugar

2 tablespoons chili powder

1 tablespoon Corky's Bar-B-Q Dry Rub

1 (1-pound) package bacon

1 bottle Corky's Bar-B-Q Sauce, Original Recipe, Smokin' Hot, or Apple

Preheat the oven to 350°F. Line a sheet pan with foil and place a wire grate on top. In a small bowl, mix together the brown sugar, chili powder, and dry rub. Rinse the chicken tenders and toss them in the spice mixture. Wrap a slice of bacon around each piece, and place on the wire grate. Bake the chicken tenders for 30 minutes, or until cooked through, basting with Bar-B-Q Sauce during the last 10 minutes of cooking.

We get our share of celebrity visitors here at Corky's. I've helped wait on Annette Bening, Jack Nicholson, and Justin Timberlake, among others. We've catered for Oprah, Rascal Flats, and American Idol. One holiday weekend, we were running around trying to handle the crazy holiday crowd. Someone phoned in a to-go order, desperate for delivery. We didn't have a spare staff member, so a friend of mine delivered the food for us. Turned out, Tom Petty had a hankering for Corky's. He gave us front row seats as a thank you.

— *Robbie Levine, Corky's employee since day one*

NANA VIDA'S VEGGIE STUFFED MUSHROOMS

"My wife's mom, known to the family as Nana Vida, was famous for her stuffed mushrooms. She was expected—no, required—to prepare them for every family event. We'd all help ourselves to spoonfuls of the filling while she was trying to stuff them," says Corky's co-owner Barry Pelts. "No matter how many she made, they were all magically consumed. Every last one, every single time. They're buttery, garlicky, and absolutely delicious."

YIELDS: 6 to 8 servings

CORKY'S FAMILY: Barry Pelts

4 (8-ounce) packages whole button mushrooms

1 cup (2 sticks) salted butter

3 teaspoons minced garlic

4 (6-ounce) cans large pitted olives, drained and chopped

1 sleeve butter crackers, crushed *(Ritz preferred)*

1 (5-ounce) container freshly shredded Parmesan cheese, divided

Remove the stems from the mushroom caps. Finely chop the stems and set the caps aside. Melt the butter in a large skillet set over medium heat. Add the garlic and sauté until fragrant, about 1 minute. Add the mushroom stems and olives and cook until the mushrooms begin to soften, about 5 minutes. Add the crackers and stir to combine. Stir in the Parmesan cheese, reserving 2 tablespoons. Reduce the heat to medium-low and cook, stirring, until the ingredients are well-combined. Remove from heat.

Preheat the oven to 350°F. Stuff the mushroom caps with the filling mixture and place on a baking sheet, filling-side up. Bake for 25 minutes, remove from the oven, and sprinkle with the reserved Parmesan. Serve warm or at room temperature.

I grew up on Corky's and, as I grew, it did, too! Maximizing every square inch of real estate at 5259 Poplar, the consistency of their fare, service, and atmosphere never fell prey to its growth and popularity. A "dry ribs" girl, I licked my Corky's-stained fingers through junior high and high school, celebrated my 21st birthday there with friends, and raised my daughters to appreciate how very special their food is. My oldest brother, Jeb, enjoys smoking BBQ at U of M tailgates, and the impending BBQ karma from the walls of the old Arcade must have rubbed off on my other brother, Jon, as he has become quite the decorated BBQ competitor. Dad is no longer with us, but we still choose Corky's when we give mom a break from the kitchen.

— *Amy Bethea, life-long customer, Memphis, TN*

LIL BO'S WINGS

Wesley, or Lil' Bo as he is known in the kitchen, and the entire Berry family have been an important part of Corky's history. Many Berry relatives have graced our doors, from the olden days up until the present. Wesley's wings have always been a "back of the house" special at employee parties.

We love these wings year-round, but come football season, watch out! These wings are always a huge hit at tailgate parties. Any dipping sauce will work, but we're partial to Corky's Ranch Bar-B-Q dip (page 33) and the Strawberry Jalapeño Bar-B-Q Sauce (page 33).

YIELDS: 12 servings

CORKY'S FAMILY: Wesley Berry

1 cup Italian dressing

1 cup sugar

1 cup hot sauce

½ cup Corky's Original Recipe Bar-B-Q Sauce

⅓ cup ketchup

¼ cup (1 stick) unsalted butter

Vegetable oil *(for frying)*

60 chicken wings or drumettes

Ranch or blue cheese dressing *(for serving)*

Carrot sticks and celery sticks *(for serving)*

To make the wing sauce, combine the dressing, sugar, hot sauce, Bar-B-Q sauce, ketchup, and butter in a large pot over low heat and cook, stirring occasionally, until the sugar and butter are melted.

In a large pot, Dutch oven, or electric fryer, heat at least 3 inches of oil to 350°F. Fry the drumettes or wings until crispy and cooked through, about 7 to 10 minutes.

Pour the wing sauce into a large bowl and toss with the cooked wings or drumettes. Allow the wings to sit in the sauce for about 10 minutes. Serve with your favorite ranch or blue cheese dressing, carrots, and celery sticks.

BILLIE'S MAGICAL MEMPHIS MEATBALLS

YIELDS: 30 to 50 meatballs

CORKY'S FAMILY: Billie Pelts

3 pounds ground beef chuck or ground beef sirloin

1 cup plain bread crumbs

1 small onion, diced

2 large eggs, lightly beaten

2 teaspoons Corky's Bar-B-Q Dry Rub

1 (38-ounce) bottle ketchup (4½ cups)

1 (18-ounce) bottle Corky's Original Recipe Bar-B-Q Sauce

1 (12-ounce) bottle chili sauce

1 lemon, juiced

In a large bowl, combine the ground beef, bread crumbs, onion, eggs, and dry rub, and mix together. (Don't overwork the meat, as that can toughen it.) Place a large pot over medium-low heat and add the ketchup, Bar-B-Q sauce, chili sauce, and lemon juice; bring to simmer. Roll the meat mixture out into meatballs and gently place in the sauce. Cook, stirring frequently so the meatballs do not stick to the bottom of the pot, until meatballs are cooked through and flavors meld, about 1 hour. Transfer to a serving bowl and serve with toothpicks.

Jenny Fenton and Billie Pelts with Danny DeVito

BLACK AND BLUE CHICKEN

The blue cheese dressing cools the heat of the seasoning, and the seasoning mellows the blueness of the cheese. Together they complement each other very nicely, making for a wonderful appetizer or entree. At one of our tasting parties, this dish drew raves from every single guest. If you don't have access to Corky's chicken, try this with any kind of smoked chicken or even a rotisserie bird.

YIELDS: 4 to 6 servings

CORKY'S FRIEND: John "Sandy" Sanders

1 pound Corky's Bar-B-Q Chicken

2 tablespoons blackened seasoning

1 cup blue cheese salad dressing

1 teaspoon finely minced garlic

Toasted French bread slices *(for serving)*

Preheat the oven to 350°F. Liberally coat the chicken with the blackened seasoning, cut the chicken into bite-size pieces, and place in a large, oven-safe serving dish. In a separate bowl, mix together the blue cheese dressing and the garlic. Pour the mixture over the chicken and toss to coat. Cover and warm in the oven until the entire mixture is heated through, taking care not to overcook. Serve with toasted French bread.

> The food we've conquered. We work daily on the consistency of service. Martha Stewart was in town this year. Fortunately, my top server was able to wait on her. She autographed the check "Excellent Service! – Martha Stewart."
>
> — *Donna Thorsen, Corky's employee for more than 15 years*

NOT LEW'S SHRIMP AND CRABMEAT DIP

This recipe originally came from Corky's manager Lew Bilbrey. Over the years, much to Lew's dismay, fellow manager Jimmy Stovall altered it by changing the main ingredient from crawfish to crabmeat. Whichever version you choose to follow will work beautifully. In the test kitchen, we favored the crawfish—I mean the crabmeat—well, it's hard to say! You'll have to be the judge. Serve the dip with baguette slices, corn chips, or in crunchy baked wonton cups, if you like.

YIELDS: 8 servings

 CORKY'S FAMILY: Jimmy Stovall

1 stick (8 tablespoons) unsalted butter

1 bunch green onions, chopped

2 tablespoons minced garlic

2 (8-ounce) packages cream cheese

1 teaspoon cayenne pepper

1 teaspoon freshly ground white pepper

1 pound jumbo lump fresh crabmeat or crawfish tails

½ pound small shrimp, cooked, deveined, and shelled

1 teaspoon Corky's Bar-B-Q Dry Rub

Baguette slices, crackers or corn chips (for serving)

Wonton wrappers (for serving; optional)

Melt the butter in a large, heavy-bottomed skillet set over medium heat. Add the onions and garlic and sauté until the onions have softened, about 5 minutes. Add the cream cheese and stir until melted. Add the cayenne pepper and white pepper, then add the seafood and stir until well mixed. Sprinkle dry rub over the top and serve warm with baguettes slices, crackers, or corn chips.

Tip: Wonton wrappers make tasty crunchy "cups" that can be filled with a variety of ingredients for an appetizer that is easy to eat with your hands and is also perfect for standing and socializing with family and friends.

To serve in wonton cups instead, preheat the oven to 350°F. Grease a mini muffin pan. Place one wonton wrapper into each muffin cup, pressing the wrapper into place. Fill each cup with dip mixture and bake about 5 minutes for a chewy wonton cup, or an additional 3 to 5 minutes for a crunchier wonton cup. Remove from the oven and let the cups cool slightly before placing on a serving platter.

LUCY'S MEXICAN CORN DIP

Lucy has been with Corky's since 1993. She started her career at the Corky's in Knoxville while attending the University of Tennessee. There she met Jimmy. They were married in 1994 and have been a long-standing Corky's family. Lucy's triplet, Eddie, is a Corky's manager.

YIELDS: 10 to 12 servings

CORKY'S FAMILY: Lucy Stovall

3 (11-ounce) cans corn with green and red bell peppers, drained (*Green Giant Mexicorn preferred*)

1 cup mayonnaise

1 cup sour cream

8 slices jalapeño pepper, diced

1 cup shredded Cheddar cheese

1 teaspoon Corky's Bar-B-Q Dry Rub

Corn chips (*for serving*)

Preheat the oven to 350°F. In a large bowl, combine the corn, mayonnaise, sour cream, and jalapeño and mix well. Pour into an oven-safe baking dish. Top with shredded Cheddar cheese and sprinkle with dry rub. Cover with foil and bake until bubbly and warmed through, about 30 minutes. Remove the foil and place under the broiler until top is browned, about 3 minutes. Serve hot with corn chips.

MS. DONNA'S PECAN CRUSTED SPINACH ARTICHOKE DIP

Since 1998, Donna Thorsen has welcomed guests to Corky's with true Southern hospitality. When the Collierville store opened, Jimmy loved her so much, he stole her away from the Cordova location. To this day, that is where you can find her.

YIELDS: 12 servings

CORKY'S FAMILY: Donna Thorsen

1 (8-ounce) package cream cheese, softened

½ cup mayonnaise

2 (9-ounce) packages frozen cream spinach, thawed

1 (14-ounce) can artichoke hearts, drained and chopped

½ cup grated Parmesan cheese

⅓ cup chopped onion

⅛ teaspoon cayenne pepper

⅓ cup crushed herb stuffing

½ cup chopped pecans

Preheat the oven to 400°F. In a large bowl, mix together the cream cheese and the mayonnaise. Stir in the spinach, artichoke hearts, cheese, onion, and cayenne pepper, and pour the mixture into a 2-quart baking dish. In a separate bowl, combine the stuffing and the pecans, and sprinkle over the dip. Bake until lightly browned on top, about 20 to 25 minutes.

What do the customers love? What do they not love?! Customers are crazy about the nachos. The pork shoulder—probably because it's fresh and moist, never dry. A lot of folks love the spaghetti—they usually get the half-and-half—half pork, half spaghetti. People love that red sauce! The ladies love the fully loaded potato. It's close to a pound, with the meat of your choice, cheese sauce, barbecue sauce. It's a solid meal, that one. Oh, can't forget the ribs. People order more ribs than anything else, and I see a preference for wet at my restaurant. Customers like to finish off with the fudge pie or the pecan pie—they're longtime favorites from the early days.

—Donna Thorsen, *Corky's employee for more than 15 years*

ROGER'S ALMOND BLUE CHEESE DIP

Roger is a Corky's spouse—his wife, Janice, manages the office at the Collierville location—and an important member of the Corky's family. They were neighbors of Amir, our Director of Operations who introduced Janice to Jimmy, and the rest is history. Janice has been with Corky's ever since.

YIELDS: 8 servings

CORKY'S FAMILY: Roger Mann

1 cup (8 ounces) sour cream

1 cup (4 ounces) slivered almonds

1 (4-ounce) package blue cheese, crumbled

¼ cup shredded Cheddar cheese

1 teaspoon soy sauce

½ teaspoon Corky's Bar-B-Q Dry Rub

Crackers or sliced apples *(for serving)*

Combine the sour cream, almonds, cheeses, soy sauce, and dry rub. Serve with your favorite crackers or spread on apple slices.

CREAMY SAUSAGE DIP

This is one of those recipes that is so easy, yet so amazingly good—and it comes from none other than our director of special events, Bonnie Phifer. Bonnie is an integral member of the Corky's team and can turn a backyard BBQ into a Southern black-tie event. Our customers count on her to give their events that special touch.

YIELDS: 8 servings

CORKY'S FAMILY: Bonnie Phifer

1 pound sausage meat

2 (8-ounce) packages cream cheese, softened

1 (10-ounce) can mixed diced tomatoes and green chiles *(Ro*tel preferred)*

Tortilla or corn chips *(for serving)*

Cook the sausage in a large, heavy bottomed skillet set over medium heat. Drain excess fat. Slowly melt the cream cheese in a double boiler. (Alternatively, use a heavy-bottom saucepan and stir frequently.) When the cheese is melted, stir in the cooked sausage and can of tomatoes and chilies. Serve in a warmed dish with tortilla or corn chips.

JOEL'S BAR-B-Q BEAN DIP

Joel has been with Corky's since the beginning. He worked his way up through the ranks and now runs our 60,000-square-foot USDA facility. We give a big thanks to Joel for making sure your grocery store shelves are stocked and the QVC orders are shipped out on time.

YIELDS: 8 servings

CORKY'S FAMILY: Joel Storck

1 small onion, chopped

¼ cup Corky's Smokin' Hot Bar-B-Q Sauce

¼ cup tomato sauce

¼ teaspoon garlic powder

1 (15-ounce) can Great Northern or other small white beans, drained, divided

4 slices bacon, cooked and crumbled

½ cup shredded Cheddar cheese

Corn chips *(for serving)*

Preheat the oven to 350°F. Place the onion, Bar-B-Q sauce, tomato sauce, garlic powder, and half of the beans in a blender and purée until smooth. Pour into a bowl and stir in the remaining beans. Spread into a baking dish and top with the bacon crumbles. Bake until heated through, about 20 minutes. Remove from the oven, sprinkle the cheese on top, and bake until cheese melts, about 5 minutes longer. Serve with corn chips.

We drive up. Corky's looks larger from the outside than it really is. Parking is a bit tough as the parking lot is small, but the smell of barbecue permeates everything. The place is packed with patrons and so we wait. To the bar we go. We enjoyed a couple of ice cold beverages, and then our table is ready. I ordered the ribs dry rubbed. The wife ordered the brisket. The ribs were smoky and not greasy in any way. Baked beans and slaw—wonderful. Same with the brisket, which comes wet with sauce over it. We left satisfied and stuffed. Would have loved to have taken part of the dessert, but no room for it. The offers on the table were the peach cobbler or the banana pudding. Oh the shame to be full. Go there when in Memphis, you will not regret it.

— *a review from Craig, Wentzville, MO*

JEFF'S SPINACH SALSA QUESO DIP

Jeff Kent started out in the early 90's as a manager at the Poplar location. He is now the production manager for our USDA facility. Jeff ensures all of our food produced for grocery stores and shipping is the same quality one would get in the restaurant.

Fresh spinach works equally well as frozen in this dip. Wash well, spin dry, and chop finely. Add the freshly chopped pieces directly to the hot dip and stir to wilt. For a spicier queso, upgrade to a hot salsa.

YIELDS: 8 servings

CORKY'S FAMILY: Jeff Kent

1 (10-ounce) package frozen chopped spinach, thawed and drained, or fresh spinach

1 pound processed cheese, cubed

1 (8-ounce) package cream cheese, cubed

1½ cups (12 ounces) salsa

¼ cup chopped cilantro

Tortilla chips *(for serving)*

Place the cheese, salsa, spinach, cream cheese, and cilantro in a microwave-safe dish and microwave in 30-second intervals, stirring to combine, until the cheeses have melted. Serve with tortilla chips.

CORKY'S BAR-B-Q POPCORN

This makes a great after-school snack and gets a bump of flavor from Corky's Bar-B-Q Dry Rub. A little goes a long way with these spices, so season lightly to your taste.

YIELDS: 3 servings

CORKY'S FRIEND: Louis Costabile

1 bag microwaveable popcorn

Melted butter *(to taste)*

Corky's Bar-B-Q Dry Rub *(to taste)*

Pop your favorite bag of popcorn according to package directions. Add the melted butter to the popcorn, if desired. Sprinkle conservatively with dry rub and toss to combine. Taste, and add more rub as desired.

REAL SWEET TEA

Sweet tea is the signature drink of the South, with roots dating back to an 1879 community cookbook. (But we bet it found its way onto Southern tables way before that!) A tall glass of this icy drink goes with every event and any menu—church suppers, family meals, ladies' luncheons, porch sittin'—you name it. Southern gatherings can be big affairs, and this sweet drink can be made in large quantities quickly and easily. Adjust the sugar to your own taste. If it's syrupy, then it's too strong. Or maybe it's just perfect. Your call.

 YIELDS: 6 to 8 servings

6 cups water

3 family-sized teabags

2 cups Simple Syrup *(page 79)*

Lemon slices *(for serving; optional)*

Bring 6 cups of water to a boil in a large pot. When the water begins to boil, remove from the heat and add the teabags. Let steep for 5 to 6 minutes.

Remove the tea bags and return the tea to the heat. Bring just to a boil, then pour into a heat-resistant pitcher and stir in simple syrup to your desired sweetness. Fill the pitcher halfway with ice, and stir until most of it melts. Fill the pitcher the rest of the way with cold water, adding more simple syrup if needed, and stir until blended. Serve over ice, with lemon slices if desired.

SIMPLE SYRUP

YIELDS: 1½ cups

1 cup water

1 cup sugar

In a small saucepan, bring the water and sugar to a boil; reduce the heat and simmer until the sugar is dissolved, about 3 minutes. Remove from heat and let cool completely. Store in a glass jar and refrigerate for up to 1 month.

FRUIT TEA

YIELDS: 12 servings

10 cups water, divided

1 cup sugar

1 stick cinnamon

3 family-size tea bags

1 (12-ounce) can frozen lemonade concentrate

1 (6-ounce) can pineapple juice

Bring 5 cups of water, the sugar, and the cinnamon to a boil for 5 minutes. Remove from the heat, add the tea bags, and allow to steep for 3 to 5 minutes. Discard the tea bags. Add the lemonade, the pineapple juice, and 5 more cups of water. Stir to combine and serve over ice.

SULTRY SUMMER PEACH TEA

YIELDS: 18 cups

4 cups water

3 family-sized tea bags

2 cups fresh mint leaves

1 (33.8-ounce) bottle peach nectar

1 (12-ounce) can frozen lemonade concentrate

½ cup Simple Syrup *(see left column)*

1 (1-liter) bottle ginger ale

1 (1-liter) bottle club soda

Fresh mint sprigs *(for serving)*

Bring 4 cups of water to a boil in a medium saucepan. Once the water is boiling, add the tea bags and the 2 cups mint leaves. Allow to boil for 1 minute and then remove from the heat. Cover and let steep for 10 minutes.

Remove and discard the tea bags and mint. Pour the liquid into a 1-gallon container. Add the peach nectar, frozen lemonade, and simple syrup. Mix well, and cover and chill for at least 8 hours or overnight.

To serve, pour the chilled mixture into a punch bowl or large dispenser. Stir in the ginger ale and club soda. Garnish with fresh mint sprigs and serve over ice for a refreshing Southern favorite.

ANN RAIFORD'S CHERRY LIMEADE

Ann has been with Corky's for more than 10 years. She always has a story for you and is known for her contagious laugh. If you have kids and visit our Corky's Poplar location, ask for Ann—she is sure to make her special Cherry Limeade for them.

YIELDS: 10 servings

CORKY'S FAMILY: Ann Raiford

1 (12-ounce) can frozen limeade concentrate

1 (2-liter) bottle lemon-lime flavored carbonated beverage

1 (10-ounce) jar maraschino cherries, drained, with juice reserved

1 medium lime, juiced

Sliced lime *(for garnish)*

Pour the can of concentrated limeade into a large pitcher and mix in the lemon-lime soda. Stir in the reserved cherry juice and the fresh lime juice. Serve over ice and garnish with the sliced lime and reserved cherries.

LAETITIA'S OLD-FASHIONED LEMONADE

There is not a story from Corky's in which Laetitia Sandler isn't a main character. Her Old Fashioned Lemonade is a customer favorite during the hot and humid Memphis summers.

YIELDS: 6 servings

CORKY'S FAMILY: Laetitia Sandler

1 recipe Simple Syrup *(page 79)*

1 cup freshly squeezed lemon juice *(from approximately 4 to 6 medium lemons)*

3 to 4 cups cold water

Sliced lemons *(for garnish)*

In a large pitcher, combine the simple syrup and the lemon juice. Add 3 to 4 cups of cold water, adjusting for desired strength. If the lemonade is too sweet for your taste, add a little more lemon juice. Refrigerate for at least 30 minutes before serving. Serve over ice and garnish with sliced lemons.

CAPT.'S LYNCHBURG LEMONADE

There's nothing like a little grown-up lemonade to quench your summertime thirst. Jack Daniels comes from Lynchburg, in our home state of Tennessee, where it's the oldest registered distillery in the country. This recipe comes from Don Pelts, the founder of Corky's and the patriarch of the family. We've always referred to him as Captain D. He truly is the captain of the ship.

YIELDS: 1 serving

¾ cup lemon-lime soda, chilled

1.5 ounces (3 tablespoons) Jack Daniels Tennessee whiskey

1.5 ounces (3 tablespoons) sweet and sour mix

1.5 ounces (3 tablespoons) triple sec or orange-flavored liqueur

Fill a tall glass with ice cubes and pour in all of the ingredients. Stir with a straw and enjoy!

ORANGE SANGRIA

This recipe came from longtime Corky's ambassador, Broady Rodgers. He passed away in 2011 and is dearly missed by all.

YIELDS: 8 servings
CORKY'S FAMILY: Broady Rodgers

1 orange

½ cup sugar

2 limes, juiced

2 cups orange juice

1 (750-milliliter) bottle dry red wine

½ cup orange liqueur

Slice the orange in half. Cut one half into thin slices and reserve for garnish. Using a vegetable peeler, remove zest in large strips from the outer peel of the other orange half. In a small bowl, combine the zest with sugar and bruise with the back of a spoon to release the oils. Combine the lime juice, orange juice, wine, and orange liqueur in a pitcher and stir in the sugar and orange zest mixture. Chill, covered, in the refrigerator, removing the orange zest after 15 minutes. Serve over ice, garnished with the reserved orange slices.

NAMI'S "NO SUBSTITUTIONS" MARGARITA

There's something about sitting by the pool on a hot summer day that just begs for an ice-cold margarita. Corky's friend Lynn Buxbaum says she makes the best one around. "Since I have been a Memphis in May International Festival and Kansas City BBQ judge for over sixteen years, this recipe has traveled with me far and wide—from the deep South to the Yankee north, east, west, and everywhere in between," Lynn says. "Once people taste this, it becomes their must-have recipe, and they join me in the tradition of passing this refreshing treat along. One key secret, though: no substitutions! After your first sip, you'll likely agree. Cheers!"

YIELDS: 4 servings

CORKY'S FRIEND: Lynn Buxbaum

1 (12-ounce) can Minute Maid Limeade frozen concentrate *(no substitutions)*

1 (12-ounce) can 7UP *(no substitutions)*

1 (12-ounce) can Miller Light beer *(no substitutions)*

8 ounces tequila

Pour frozen limeade into a glass pitcher. Slowly add 7UP and Miller Light. Swirl tequila in limeade container to rinse and then pour into pitcher. Mix together.
Serve over ice.

BAR-B-Q MARY

Jan has been with Corky's for more than 20 years. She started, like the rest of us, in the drive-thru. Now she oversees our successful mail-order division. When you want to treat your friends and family across the country to Corky's world-famous barbecue, Jan is the person to know!

For extra zip at your next brunch, coat the rim of your Bloody Mary glass with Corky's dry rub like we do here at Corky's. A shot of barbecue sauce in the drink adds another level of flavor beyond the usual tomato and celery.

YIELDS: 3 to 4 servings

CORKY'S FAMILY: Jan Klein

1¼ cups tomato or
vegetable juice

5 ounces vodka

1 lemon, juiced

2 tablespoons Corky's
Smokin' Hot Bar-B-Q Sauce

1 tablespoon prepared
horseradish

2 teaspoons
Worcestershire sauce

½ teaspoon celery salt

1 (2.5-ounce) bottle
Corky's Bar-B-Q Dry Rub

Celery, jumbo green olives,
or pickled green beans
(for garnish)

Combine the tomato juice, vodka, lemon juice, Bar-B-Q sauce, horseradish, Worcestershire sauce, and celery salt in a large pitcher to make the Bloody Mary mixture.

Pour the dry rub onto a small plate. Moisten the rim of a glass and dip the rim into the dry rub. Fill a highball or martini glass with ice and pour in Bloody Mary mixture. Garnish the drink with celery, jumbo green olives, or pickled green beans.

EVERETT'S KICKED-BACK LIME COOLER

Everett Dennis has been with Corky's since the beginning. He is the manager we turn to for all new store openings. Corky's would not be Corky's without Everett Dennis.

YIELDS: 6 servings

CORKY'S FAMILY: Everett Dennis

1½ cups pineapple juice

1½ cups vodka

3 tablespoons freshly squeezed lime juice *(from approximately 2 limes)*

1 cup pineapple chunks

1 cup sugar

4 medium lime wedges, plus 6 more *(for garnish)*

Mix the pineapple juice, vodka, and lime juice in a large pitcher and chill until cold. Thread the pineapple chunks onto 6 small skewers.

Pour the sugar onto a large plate. Moisten the rims of serving glasses by rubbing them with the lime wedges, and dip the rims of the glasses in the sugar. Place a pineapple skewer in each glass, fill with the vodka mixture, and serve. Garnish each with an additional lime wedge.

PERFECT ARNOLD PALMER

The South is hot and humid during the summer months. Nothing hits the spot more than a refreshing ice-cold lemony tea, and it's a top request by Corky's diners trying to recover from the Memphis heat. This popular concoction gets its name from the famous golfer Arnold Palmer, who makes these his go-to for summertime cool.

YIELDS: 1 serving

1 cup brewed tea

1 cup Old Fashioned Lemonade *(page 81)*

1 slice fresh lemon *(for garnish)*

Fill a tall glass with ice. Pour in the tea and the lemonade. If you like it sweet, use Real Sweet Tea (page 78) instead of unsweetened tea for your Arnold Palmer. Garnish with a lemon slice and enjoy.

PORCH SITTIN' MINT JULEPS

Miss Annie was a kitchen staple from the day the doors opened until her retirement a few years ago. Miss Annie had one speed and that was slow, but one thing you could always count on was that her BBQ sandwich would be the absolute best sandwich ever. This recipe for cool, smooth, slow-sippin' Mint Julep, intended to be enjoyed slowly, reminds us of Miss Annie, the perfect sandwich, and her calm, laid-back style.

YIELDS: 10 to 12 servings

CORKY'S FAMILY: Miss Annie

12 lemons

12 cups water

1 cup loosely packed fresh mint leaves, plus additional for garnish

3 to 4 cups Simple Syrup *(page 79)*

3 to 4 cups bourbon, or more to taste

Juice the lemons, setting aside the rinds and the juice. In a medium saucepan, combine the rinds with 12 cups of water and 1 cup of mint leaves and simmer for 15 minutes. (Do not allow the mixture to boil.) Remove from the heat and strain, discarding the mint and lemon rinds. In a large pitcher, combine the lemon mixture, lemon juice, and simple syrup to taste. Stir in the bourbon, and add more if desired. (Some have been known to, ahem, double or even triple the bourbon.) The recipe can be made ahead and refrigerated. Serve in chilled julep cups packed with ice, and garnish with additional mint.

SALADS, SOUPS, & SANDWICHES

CRISP GREENS FOR HOT DAYS, WARM SOUPS FOR COLD NIGHTS, *HEARTY* BAR-B-QUE SALADS FOR EMPTY BELLIES AND *simple yet scrumptious* SANDWICHES WHEN EASY-PEASY SOUNDS ABSOLUTELY PERFECT.

BLT Pasta Salad

Bar-B-Q Chicken
and Sausage Gumbo

Uncle Doug's Bar-B-Q
Stuffed Burgers

John's Smokin' Bar-B-Q Bologna

Watermelon Salad with Feta

BAR-B-Q CHEF SALAD

The Bar-B-Q Ranch Dipping Sauce and Dressing (page 33) makes this salad.

YIELDS: 4 to 6 servings

CORKY'S FAMILY: Jimmy Stovall

1 small head romaine
lettuce, chopped

1 small head iceberg
lettuce, chopped

1 cup shredded cabbage

1 cup shredded carrots (*from
about 2 to 3 medium carrots*)

1 pound Corky's Bar-B-Q Pulled
Pork or Chicken

1 (16-ounce) jar whole
pepperoncini peppers, drained

1 small red onion, sliced
into rings

2 large eggs, hard-boiled, peeled,
and sliced

1 recipe Bar-B-Q Ranch
Dipping Sauce and Dressing
(*page 33*)

In a large bowl, toss together the lettuces, cabbage, and carrots. Top with the meat, peppers, onion rings, and hard-boiled egg slices. Serve with Bar-B-Q Ranch dressing.

When Corky's opened in Memphis, there was a love affair between my dad and their pork until he breathed his last. BBQ was a culinary thread woven through his life and, subsequently, mine. Dad proposed marriage to my mom at the drive-in at Leonard's BBQ on South Bellevue during the mid-1950s. My parents enjoyed meals at Leonard's, Pig & Whistle, The Rendezvous, TOPS, and Gridley's, but it was Corky's that ultimately set the gold standard in pork. Any time mom took the night off from cooking her usual scratch fare, dad would opt for grilling on the patio or heading to Corky's—rarely missing a side of decadent onion rings. And the rolls—don't forget the rolls with their apple BBQ sauce!

— *Amy Bethea, life-long customer, Memphis, TN*

BLT PASTA SALAD

Around here in the Mid-South, the BLT is almost as important as the Bar-B-Q Sandwich. This recipe transforms the flavors of a classic BLT into a fresh pasta salad—and a sure favorite for the entire family.

YIELDS: 8 to 10 servings
CORKY'S FAMILY: Carol Sweeney

1 (16-ounce) box farfalle (bow-tie) pasta

1 head romaine lettuce

½ cup milk

½ cup mayonnaise

1 (0.4-ounce) package ranch salad dressing mix (*Hidden Valley Ranch preferred*)

2 cups cherry tomatoes, sliced in half

8 ounces center-cut bacon (about 12 slices), cooked and crumbled

1 bunch green onions, sliced
(*about ¾ cup*)

Salt and freshly ground black pepper
(*to taste*)

Fill a large pot with lightly salted water and bring to a rolling boil over high heat. Add the pasta and cook until al dente. Drain well. Wash and chop the lettuce.

In a small bowl, whisk the milk, mayonnaise, and ranch mix. In a large bowl, toss the cooked pasta, lettuce, tomatoes, bacon, and green onions together. Add the dressing and toss to combine. Season to taste with salt and freshly ground black pepper.

MEEMA'S PASTA SALAD

YIELDS: 8 to 10 servings
CORKY'S FRIEND: Ray Woodward

1 (12-ounce) package tri-color pasta
(*Ronzoni Radiatore preferred*)

**1 pint grape tomatoes,
cut in half**

**1 (15-ounce) can chickpeas
or garbanzo beans, drained**

1 green bell pepper, diced

1 small onion, diced
(*about 1 cup*)

1 (8-ounce) package sharp Cheddar cheese, cubed

1 (6-ounce) can black olives, drained

1 (5-ounce) package mini pepperoni

1 (5-ounce) package garlic and cheese croutons

1 (0.7-ounce) package Italian salad dressing mix (*Good Seasons preferred*)

Fill a large pot with lightly salted water and bring to a rolling boil over high heat. Cook the pasta until al dente. Drain in a colander, and rinse with cold water.

When cool, transfer the pasta to a large bowl. Add the tomatoes, chickpeas, pepper, onion, cheese, olives, pepperoni, and croutons and toss to combine. Prepare the Italian salad dressing according to the package instructions and pour over the salad. Toss well and serve.

BLT Pasta Salad

HEIRLOOM TOMATO SALAD

Michelle Musolf married into the Corky's family. Her husband Bob and brother-in-law Paul are known as the Corky's Comedians. If there is a prank pulled or a joke made, you can bet Bob, Paul, or both have something to do with it.

Heirloom tomatoes have flavor in spades and add such beautiful colors to the plate. If you have access to any specialty tomatoes, this is the recipe to let them shine. Prepare it for a potluck or backyard barbecue.

YIELDS: 4 servings

CORKY'S FAMILY: Michelle Musolf

1 pound various heirloom tomatoes, chopped (about 2 cups)

2 medium (1-ounce) shallots, minced (about ½ cup)

1 garlic clove, minced

1 tablespoon olive oil

1 tablespoon aged balsamic vinegar

Salt and freshly ground black pepper (to taste)

Several fresh basil leaves, torn

Combine the tomatoes, shallots, and garlic. Add the olive oil and vinegar and gently toss to combine. Season to taste with salt and pepper. Garnish with the fresh basil leaves.

We drove from Texas to New York and this, ladies and gentlemen, was the best out of the dozens of BBQ we tasted throughout our journey. I ordered the wet traditional ribs, which were seasoned to perfection and fell right off the bone. My mom ordered the BBQ nachos. Man, these were a heart attack on a plate! They were piled high with cheese, meat, barbecue sauce and a flag proudly stating "Corky's" on the top. We couldn't finish these because it was so much food. It was really good and I could see why it was award-winning. My grandmother got the bar-b-q pork sandwich, which is also award-winning. It was good—juicy, tasty, and flavorful. But she was too busy eating my ribs to enjoy hers much! So, if you are coming here, you NEED to get the ribs. They are fantastic! If you can't make a trip to Memphis, you can always order them online. We took two pounds to go as Christmas gifts for our friends. Needless to say, our friends loved them just as much as we did!

— a review from Kate, Flower Mound, TX

LAUREN'S AUTUMN BERRY CHICKEN SALAD

The roasted chicken makes this chicken salad stand out from the crowd. The chicken is utterly tender and flavorful and complements the other ingredients. The cranberries add a touch of sweet-tart goodness, and the crunch of the pecans and celery make it positively scrumptious. For a smoky (and delicious) variation, use 3 cups Corky's Pulled Smoked Chicken instead of roasted chicken and add salt only if needed.

YIELDS: 8 servings

CORKY'S FRIEND: Lauren Edmonds

Roasted Chicken

2 pounds split chicken breasts *(bone in, skin on)*

1 tablespoon olive oil

1 teaspoon kosher or sea salt

½ teaspoon freshly ground black pepper

Chicken Salad

⅓ cup mayonnaise

2 tablespoons extra-virgin olive oil

3 teaspoons country-style Dijon mustard

2 teaspoons apple cider vinegar

2 teaspoons honey

1½ teaspoons kosher or sea salt

2 celery stalks, sliced into ¼-inch-thick half moons *(about 1 cup)*

½ cup sweetened dried cranberries

½ cup chopped pecans

For roasted chicken: Preheat the oven to 400°F and place the chicken in a glass baking dish. Drizzle both sides with olive oil, and sprinkle with salt and pepper. Roast skin-side up, uncovered, on the middle rack until the internal temperature reaches 165 degrees, about 40 to 45 minutes.

Remove from the oven and let cool completely. Remove the skin and bones from the chicken breast and shred the meat with your hands into bite-size pieces. This should yield about 3 cups of shredded chicken meat.

For chicken salad: Whisk together the mayonnaise, olive oil, mustard, vinegar, honey, and salt in a large bowl. Combine the mayonnaise mixture with the prepared chicken, celery, cranberries, and pecans, and mix well. Cover and refrigerate at least 30 minutes. (This recipe is best if made a day ahead.)

Watermelon Salad with Feta and Vinaigrette

WATERMELON SALAD WITH FETA AND VINAIGRETTE

YIELDS: 8 to 10 servings

CORKY'S FRIEND: Julia Rutland

4 cups cut watermelon balls or chunks

½ cup chopped red onion *(from about ½ small onion)*

2 tablespoons chopped fresh basil

2 tablespoons balsamic vinegar

1 tablespoon olive oil

Salt and freshly ground black pepper *(to taste)*

⅓ cup *(about 1⅓ ounces)* **crumbled feta cheese**

Combine the watermelon, onion, and basil in a large bowl. In a small bowl, whisk together the vinegar and oil. Pour the vinaigrette over the watermelon and toss to combine. Season to taste with salt and pepper. Top with feta and refrigerate until ready to serve.

Note: Fresh mint is a great substitute for basil.

QUICK AND EASY CORN SALAD

Everyone loves this side dish, and it couldn't be easier. Win-win!

YIELDS: 6 servings

CORKY'S FRIEND: Connie Page

1 (15.25-ounce) can whole-kernel yellow corn, drained

1 (11-ounce) can white shoepeg corn, drained

1 (10-ounce) can diced tomatoes and green chilies, drained *(Ro*Tel preferred)*

¼ cup mayonnaise

1 small onion, chopped *(about 1 cup)*

Salt and freshly ground black pepper *(to taste)*

In a large bowl, combine the corn, tomatoes and chilies mixture, and mayonnaise. Add enough of the onion to suit your taste. Season to taste with salt and pepper. Cover and refrigerate overnight.

SHOUT HALLELUJAH POTATO SALAD

Our friends at the Yoknapatawpha Arts Council graciously shared this dish from their cookbook, *Square Table*. It won the coveted Southern Foodways Alliance award in the potato salad competition, so you can imagine how good it'll be on your buffet table.

YIELDS: 10 to 12 servings

CORKY'S FRIEND: Wayne Andrews

5 pounds small Yukon Gold potatoes

5 eggs, hard-boiled, peeled, and chopped

1 (4-ounce) jar diced pimentos, drained

4 dashes hot sauce *(Louisiana preferred)*

4 celery stalks, chopped *(about 2 cups)*

1½ cups chopped red onion *(from about 1 medium onion)*

1½ cups chopped green bell pepper *(from about 2 green bell peppers)*

1¼ cups chopped fresh parsley

1¼ cups yellow mustard

1⅛ cups mayonnaise

1 cup sweet salad cube pickles *(see note)*

¼ cup seasoned rice vinegar

1 or 2 jalapeño peppers, seeded and minced

1 tablespoon olive oil

2 teaspoons celery salt

Salt and freshly ground black pepper *(to taste)*

Paprika *(for garnish)*

Bring a large pot of salted water to a boil and cook the potatoes until tender, about 20 minutes. Drain in a colander and peel off the skins with your fingers under cold running water. When the potatoes are cool, chop into small pieces and transfer to a large mixing bowl. Add the eggs. In a small bowl, mix the pimentos with the hot sauce and add to the potato mixture. Add the celery, onion, peppers, parsley, mustard, mayonnaise, pickles, vinegar, jalapeños, olive oil, and celery salt, but do not stir. Mix by hand, mashing some potatoes and leaving others in chunks. Season to taste with salt and pepper. Serve in a bowl or mound on a serving platter. Dust with paprika. Cover and refrigerate 3 to 4 hours. Can be made one day ahead of time.

Note: Sweet salad cube pickles can be found in the pickle section of your super market. Pickle relish can be substituted.

OLD FASHIONED POTATO SALAD

When Mona joined the Corky's accounting office there were two people: Mona and Poncie, Don Pelts' father. Now Mona runs the department with eight full-time staff members.

YIELDS: 8 servings

CORKY'S FAMILY: Mona Ashcraft

2 pounds new potatoes

½ cup sliced green onions *(from about 6 green onions)*

2 eggs, hard-boiled, peeled, and chopped

¼ cup chopped dill pickles

Corky's Bar-B-Q Dry Rub *(to taste)*

½ cup mayonnaise

½ cup Dijon mustard

Salt and freshly ground black pepper *(to taste)*

Bring a large pot of salted water to a boil and cook the potatoes until tender. Allow to cool in a large bowl, then crush the potatoes with your fingers, leaving the skins on. Add the green onions, eggs, and dill pickles, and season to taste with dry rub. In a small bowl, combine the mayonnaise and mustard. Pour over the potato mixture and toss gently to coat. Season to taste with salt and pepper. Cover and refrigerate until ready to serve.

I could tell you a lot about our competitors, and I'm friends with a lot of them. I could eat there on certain days and think their barbecue is as good as ours. (This is Memphis, after all.) But if you go there 10 times in a row, will their barbecue be consistent?

— *Barry Pelts, co-owner*

101

SALLY BILBREY'S CHICKEN SALAD

If Corky's Chicken is unavailable, you can substitute any shredded cooked chicken and ½ teaspoon of salt.

YIELDS: 8 servings
CORKY'S FAMILY: Lew Bilbrey

¾ cups mayonnaise

⅓ cup sliced chives *(from about 1 bunch chives)*

1 teaspoon yellow or Dijon mustard

½ teaspoon curry powder or ginger

3 cups Corky's Bar-B-Q Pulled Chicken

1½ cups red seedless grapes, sliced in half

1 cup sliced celery *(from about 2 celery stalks)*

½ cup chopped pecans or walnuts

Whisk mayonnaise, chives, mustard, and curry powder in a large bowl to blend. Add the chicken, grapes, celery, and nuts and toss to coat. Cover and refrigerate at least 3 hours.

> In Memphis, barbecue is just hometown cooking. I've got some customers who come in three to four times a week.
>
> — *Lew Bilbrey, manager*
> *Corky's Collierville*

CORN, PEA, AND GREEN BEAN SALAD

YIELDS: 8 to 12 servings
CORKY'S FRIEND: Amy Newsom

2 (15-ounce) cans very young small early peas, drained *(LeSueur preferred)*

2 (11-ounce) cans white shoepeg corn, drained

1 (14.5-ounce) can French-style green beans, drained

½ medium red onion, diced *(about ¾ cup)*

1 (4-ounce) jar diced pimentos, drained

½ cup apple cider vinegar

½ cup sugar

¼ cup vegetable oil

1 teaspoon freshly ground black pepper

Combine the peas, corn, green beans, onion, and pimentos in a large bowl. In a medium saucepan, combine the vinegar, sugar, and oil and bring to a boil. Cook until the sugar has dissolved, about 3 to 5 minutes, and then pour over the vegetable mixture. Add the pepper and toss to coat. Let cool, and then cover and refrigerate overnight. Serve chilled or at room temperature.

JOSH'S SMOKEY BAR-B-Q BACON BURGER 🔥

Try topping this burger with the Blue Cheese and Bacon Slaw (page 121) for a rich accompaniment to the grilled meat.

YIELDS: 4 servings

CORKY'S FAMILY: Josh Woodman

1 pound ground sirloin

2 tablespoons Corky's Bar-B-Q Dry Rub

1 (18-ounce) bottle Corky's Original Recipe Bar-B-Q Sauce

4 slices sharp Cheddar cheese

4 slices bacon, cooked

1 cup coleslaw

4 hamburger buns

Prepare a charcoal or gas grill for medium-heat cooking. Lightly mix the ground sirloin with the dry rub and form into 4 equal patties.

Grill the patties, basting them with some of the Bar-B-Q sauce, until they reach the desired doneness. Add one cheese slice atop each burger to melt. Remove the burgers from the grill and top with cooked bacon, extra Bar-B-Q sauce, and slaw. Serve on toasted hamburger buns.

UNCLE DOUG'S
BAR-B-Q STUFFED BURGERS

"I absolutely love juicy pulled pork from Corky's and fresh-off-the grill Black Angus burgers," says Douglas. "One Saturday afternoon, I was experimenting on the grill and combined the two, and in the process created one of the best burgers I have ever made. They were an instant hit! Be sure to keep the recipe handy, because everyone will be asking for a copy."

YIELDS: 8 servings

CORKY'S FRIEND: Douglas Gage

2 pounds ground Black Angus beef

½ pound Corky's Bar-B-Q Pulled Pork, chopped

¾ cup Corky's Original Recipe Bar-B-Q sauce *(plus additional sauce for serving)*

½ cup finely chopped onion *(from about ½ small onion)*

Corky's Bar-B-Q Dry Rub *(to taste)*

8 hamburger buns

Coleslaw *(for serving; use your favorite recipe)*

Prepare a grill for medium-high heat cooking. Combine and thoroughly mix the meats, ¾ cup Bar-B-Q sauce, and onion. Form 8 burgers and lightly sprinkle each side of the patties with dry rub. Grill, watching closely as the Bar-B-Q sauce can quickly lead to charred burgers. Serve on buns and top with coleslaw and additional sauce.

When I was 15, my dad made me work three days a week—two nights and one weekend day or night. Just like a regular part-timer. Also like a regular, I had to ask ahead of time if I needed time off. I almost missed getting confirmed at the temple because I forgot to ask off. It didn't matter that I was the owner's daughter. In fact, that made it even more important to him that I show up on time, follow all the rules, and do a good job.

— *Tricia Woodman, daughter of Corky's founder*

SMOKIN' APPLE TURKEY BURGER

Corky's Apple Bar-B-Q Sauce adds loads of flavor to the lean ground turkey in this burger. Serve with the Apple Coleslaw (page 122), a delicious side.

YIELDS: 4 servings
CORKY'S FAMILY: Daniel Turner

1 pound lean ground turkey

½ cup Corky's Apple Bar-B-Q Sauce, divided

⅓ cup plain bread crumbs

Hickory wood or chips *(for smoking)*

4 large hamburger buns

In a large bowl, mix together the ground turkey, ¼ cup of the Bar-B-Q sauce, and bread crumbs. Divide the mixture into four equal parts and form into patties.

Light the charcoal in an outdoor grill. Allow it to develop a light coating of gray ash, about 25 to 30 minutes, with the temperature reaching 350°F. Add the burgers to the grill and cook using indirect heat. Add the hickory wood to the coals and close the lid. Monitor your burgers, allowing them to cook thoroughly. Turn burgers occasionally, brushing on additional Bar-B-Q sauce for extra flavor. Serve on the hamburger buns.

BARRY'S PULLED BAR-B-Q CHICKEN WRAP

Barry Pelts, the co-owner of Corky's, is an absolute sucker for this wrap—it includes all his favorite ingredients, rolled up into one tortilla to go.

YIELDS: 1 serving
CORKY'S FAMILY: Barry Pelts

1 large tortilla

1 large leaf Romaine lettuce

¼ pound Corky's Bar-B-Q Chicken

Shredded pepper jack cheese *(to taste)*

Chopped tomato *(to taste)*

Diced red onion *(to taste)*

Corky's Original Bar-B-Q Sauce *(to taste)*

Line the tortilla with the lettuce leaf and fill with the pulled chicken and desired amounts of the cheese, tomato, and onion. Drizzle with the desired amount of Bar-B-Q sauce. Fold the bottoms of the tortilla up, and roll up the wrap tightly. Serve immediately, or wrap in plastic wrap and refrigerate until ready to serve.

The culture that my dad built is what separates us from the rest. We assume that everything is going to screw up. If my bun toaster breaks, I have two back-ups. If the neon on the sign goes out, we have a rule you have to call a manager immediately. We really focus a lot of attention on the drive-thru. We have a manager checking every order. If you get home and find something wrong with an order, we will deliver the correct thing to your home. We serve four to six thousand people a day. We maybe get one order wrong per day. I'd say that's a pretty good record.

— *Barry Pelts, co-owner*

BAR-B-Q SANDWICH

In Memphis, if someone says, "Come on over for a barbecue sandwich," they are referring to the king of all sandwiches. Namely, pulled pork topped with coleslaw and barbecue sauce, served on a warm bun. Here are some of our favorite sandwich combinations for a quick, easy, and delicious meal that the entire family will love.

THE BASICS: Corky's Bar-B-Q Pulled Pork | Sandwich buns | Slaw | Bar-B-Q sauce

LAYNE'S SPECIAL — Pulled pork served as sliders on Corky's rolls or open-faced on Texas toast, with a helping of Mary Dee's Cole Slaw (page 121) and a drizzle of Corky's Smokin' Hot Bar-B-Q Sauce on top, and Miss Tootie's Bar-B-Que Beans (page 137) on the side.

BRANDON'S SPECIAL — Pulled pork served on hoagie rolls with Apple Coleslaw (page 122) and a glug of Corky's Apple Bar-B-Q Sauce on top, with Black Dog's Beer Baked Beans (page 132) served on the side.

SHARON'S SPECIAL — Pulled pork served on hamburger buns, topped with plenty of Corky's Original Recipe Bar-B-Q Sauce and ample Buttermilk Coleslaw (page 125), served with Classic Memphis Baked Beans (page 131) on the side.

QVC Host Sharon Faetsch grabbing a bite of her favorite Memphis Bar-B-Q backstage!

For Southerners "...pimento cheese can mean a little comfort, a little memory, a lot of peace. However your grandmother made it. Dig in."

— Kendra Myers, Southern Foodways Alliance
Pimento Cheese Invitational cookbook.

AUNT ROSIE'S GRILLED PIMENTO CHEESE SANDWICH

The only thing better than a grilled cheese sandwich is a grilled pimento cheese sandwich. Jimmy and Lucy, who have both worked at Corky's since their teens, consider this a staple for quick family dinners with their kids.

"For as long as I can remember, Jimmy's Aunt Rosie made the best pimento cheese, always shredded fine. I believe what sets hers apart from all the rest is the hard boiled eggs," says Lucy. "Whenever she visited, the first thing she would do is make a big batch of her pimento cheese. And the best part is, right before she left, she would make another batch—made fresh for us to remember her by."

YIELDS: 4 servings

CORKY'S FAMILY: Lucy Stovall

2 cups (8 ounces) finely grated mild Cheddar cheese

2 large eggs, hard-boiled, peeled, and finely grated

1 (7-ounce) jar pimentos, drained and chopped

1½ tablespoons mayonnaise

½ tablespoon freshly ground black pepper

1 loaf French bread, cut into 1-inch slices

2 tablespoons unsalted butter, softened

In a large bowl, mix together the Cheddar, eggs, pimentos, mayonnaise, and pepper. Chill. Make sandwiches with a thick smear of the pimento cheese. Butter the outside of the sandwiches with softened butter. Set a large skillet over medium-high heat and cook the sandwiches, turning once, until toasted.

For grill marks on your sandwich like the photo, toast on medium heat grill or a grill pan set over medium heat on the stove until grill marks form and the cheese melts.

JOHN'S SMOKIN' BAR-B-Q BOLOGNA 🔥

Barbecued bologna is classic old-school Memphis eats, especially at Sweeney backyard cookouts. For extra-good flavor, pan grill the bologna for a few minutes before putting it on the sandwich.

YIELDS: 10 to 12 sandwiches

CORKY'S FAMILY: John Sweeney

5 pounds whole bologna, uncut

1 (18-ounce) bottle Corky's Original Bar-B-Q sauce

¼ Cup spicy brown mustard

1 (12-ounce) bottle chili sauce *(such as Heinz)*

1½ loaves thick-slice white bread or 12 hamburger buns, toasted

Prepare your smoker with hickory wood and bring it to 235°F. In a medium saucepan, combine the barbecue sauce, chili sauce, and mustard, stirring often until it comes to a simmer, and then remove from the heat.

Place the bologna on a cutting board and remove the red skin wrapper. Using a chef's knife, score the top of bologna in a diamond pattern, cutting at least halfway through the meat, but not all the way. Place the bologna in a large aluminum pan, cover with the Bar-B-Q sauce mixture, and roll in the sauce to coat completely.

Place the bologna in the smoker and smoke for 3 hours, tending the fire to keep it at a steady 235°F. After 3 hours, carefully remove the pan from smoker and generously baste the bologna with the sauce, taking care to get it down into the slices. Return the pan to the smoker for another hour. Once the sauce has caramelized, remove from smoker and transfer the bologna to a cutting board. Loosely tent with foil and let rest for at least 5 minutes. Slice and serve on buttered Texas Toast or your favorite bun.

EDDIE'S-STYLE HOT DOG

Eddie Gavin has been with Corky's since the 1980s (he started when he was just a young 'un). Through the years, he has worked every position and has managed three of the Memphis stores. Eddie is definitely the guy you want next to you when the Bar-B-Q hits the fan!

YIELDS: 8 servings
CORKY'S FAMILY: Eddie Gavin

1 (16-ounce) package hot dogs

1 bottle Corky's Bar-B-Q Sauce *(Original Recipe or Smokin' Hot)*

1 (12- or 16-ounce) package hot dog buns

Coleslaw *(for serving; use your favorite recipe)*

Hot dog condiments *(for serving; use all of your favorites)*

Prepare a grill for medium-heat cooking. Coat the hot dogs with the Bar-B-Q sauce and grill. Serve with the buns, coleslaw, and your favorite hot dog condiments.

Don't forget to slaw the dog!

FRANK'S SAUSAGE SANDWICH

Frank stared his career in Bar-B-Q with another Memphis eatery, but he realized early on that if he wanted to be part of a world-famous Bar-B-Q joint, he needed to join the Corky's team. He did, and Frank now oversees quality control at our USDA facility.

YIELDS: 1 serving
CORKY'S FAMILY: Frank Sala

1 tablespoon oil

¼ cup thinly sliced onion

¼ cup thinly sliced green bell pepper

1 smoked sausage, grilled

1 hoagie roll

Corky's Smokin' Hot Bar-B-Q Sauce *(to taste)*

In a small heavy-bottomed skillet over medium heat, heat the oil. Add the onion and pepper and sauté until they are soft and the onion is translucent. Place the grilled sausage link in your favorite roll or bun, top with the onion and pepper mixture, and add Corky's Smokin' Hot Bar-B-Q Sauce to taste. Serve piping hot.

BRUNSWICK STEW

Calling all meat lovers: This is the stew for you. If you're trying to find a good use for some leftovers like pulled pork, beef brisket, or barbecued chicken, they can find a lovely home in this rich soup. You can also substitute rotisserie chicken.

YIELDS: 12 servings

CORKY'S FAMILY: Tony Boyd

½ cup (1 stick) salted butter

1 large sweet onion, finely diced *(about 2 cups)*

1 tablespoon minced garlic

2 tablespoons Worcestershire sauce

1½ teaspoons salt

1½ teaspoons freshly ground black pepper

½ teaspoon cayenne pepper

½ cup Corky's Original Recipe Bar-B-Q Sauce

½ pound Corky's Bar-B-Q Pulled Chicken

½ pound Corky's Bar-B-Q Beef Brisket, chopped

½ pound smoked sausage, sliced

½ pound Corky's Bar-B-Q Pork Shoulder, pulled or chopped

1 (28-ounce) can plus 1 (15-ounce) can crushed tomatoes

1 (15.25-ounce) can corn

1 (15-ounce) can lima beans

2 cups chicken stock

Hot crusty bread *(for serving)*

Melt the butter in a large saucepan over medium heat. Add the onion and garlic and sauté until the onion is translucent, about 15 minutes. Stir in the Worcestershire sauce, salt, black pepper, and cayenne. Simmer 5 minutes and add the Bar-B-Q sauce. Stir in the chicken, beef, sausage, and pork. Add the tomatoes, corn, and lima beans. Stir in the chicken stock and let the stew simmer over medium heat 30 minutes. Serve with hot crusty bread.

If you go to one rib joint in Memphis, this is it! Do not waste your time anywhere else, like we did. I have never had as good a rib anytime, anywhere, in the world. The quality of the meat was amazing. No fat at all. I had the half wet/half dry rub for two and shared it with my husband. The most amazing dry rub—delicious. Tender, fall-off-the-bone meat. Beans were average, slaw was better than average. Rolls were fantastic. Service was excellent—had to wait about 40 minutes on Friday night, but I'd wait even longer. This is the place! Corky's. Now I will crave this until the next time I return to Memphis.

— *a review from YF, Smyrna, GA*

BAR-B-Q CHICKEN AND SAUSAGE GUMBO

As with most soups and stews, this gumbo tastes much better on day two or three, after the flavors have had time to meld. If you do not have Corky's Pulled Chicken, you can use a rotisserie chicken or any cooked, pulled chicken.

YIELDS: 6 servings

CORKY'S FAMILY: Samuel Ford

⅓ cup all-purpose flour

⅓ cup vegetable oil

½ cup chopped onion *(from about ½ small onion)*

½ cup chopped green or red bell pepper *(from about ½ pepper)*

½ cup sliced celery *(from about 1 celery stalk)*

3 garlic cloves, minced

2 tablespoons Cajun seasoning

1¾ cups (14 ounces) beef broth

¾ cup water

1¼ cups (10 ounces) frozen cut okra

1½ cups Corky's Bar-B-Q Pulled Chicken

1 (8-ounce) cooked smoked sausage, sliced

Steamed rice *(for serving)*

Begin by making the roux: In a 3-quart heavy saucepan over medium-high heat, combine the flour and oil, whisking until smooth. Cook for 5 minutes, stirring constantly. Reduce the heat to medium. Continue cooking and stirring constantly until the roux is dark reddish-brown, about 8 to 10 minutes longer.

Stir in the onion, pepper, celery, and garlic. Cook until vegetables are tender, stirring frequently, about 10 minutes. Stir in the Cajun seasoning and follow with the broth and ¾ cup water. Add the okra. Bring to a boil, and then reduce heat and simmer, covered, for 15 minutes. Stir in the chicken and sausage and cook until heated through. Ladle over rice to serve.

My dad never stopped. He had a vision of what he wanted in a restaurant and he believed in treating his employees right. People grow into their positions. Bussers to servers, servers to managers, managers to general managers. Hire from within and promote from within, he says. It works for us—most of our management team has been with us for 20 years.

— *Tricia Woodman, daughter of Corky's founder*

BEANS & SLAW

WITH **MEMPHIS** BARBEQUE, YOU'RE WELCOME TO SERVE <u>ANY</u> GOOD **SOUTHERN** SIDES YOU LIKE, AS LONG AS EVERY <u>PLATE</u> INCLUDES **BEANS & SLAW** ♥. SERIOUSLY—THIS IS HOW IT WORKS HERE, AND YOU'LL BE DOING **CORKY'S** A _major_ INJUSTICE IF YOU FAIL TO HOLD TRUE TO THESE MOST _SACRED of SIDES_ ★

Spinach Coleslaw

Beans with a kick

SLAWS

Mary Dee's Seasoned Cole Slaw

MARY DEE'S SEASONED COLE SLAW

"Every time I visited my aunt in Memphis, she would whip up this recipe," says Mary. "Just reading it reminds me of her great Southern hospitality and the slaw's tangy, delicious flavor. She'd be tickled pink to see this in print!"

YIELDS: 10 servings
CORKY'S FRIEND: Mary Dee Richmond

1 cup mayonnaise

⅓ cup sugar

2 tablespoons Dijon mustard

2 tablespoons apple cider vinegar

1 tablespoon celery seed

½ teaspoon salt

½ teaspoon freshly ground white pepper

½ teaspoon freshly ground black pepper

½ cup diced green bell pepper (from about ½ large pepper)

2 tablespoons diced white onion

2 (16-ounce) packages coleslaw mix with carrots

To make the dressing, combine the mayonnaise, sugar, mustard, vinegar, celery seed, salt, and ground peppers in a small bowl. Whisk until the dressing is smooth. Stir in the bell pepper and onion. Refrigerate the dressing until ready to use.

Just before serving, empty the coleslaw mix into a large bowl. Add the dressing a little at a time, mixing until nicely coated but not overdressed.

BLUE CHEESE AND BACON SLAW

Salty bacon pairs beautifully with creamy blue cheese for a unique slaw that is delicious with steaks or on a grilled burger.

YIELDS: 8 servings
CORKY'S FAMILY: Carol Sweeney

1 (16-ounce) package coleslaw mix

4 slices bacon, cooked and crumbled

½ cup (2 ounces) crumbled blue cheese

1 cup ranch dressing

¼ teaspoon freshly ground black pepper

In a large bowl combine the coleslaw mix, bacon, and blue cheese. Add ranch dressing and pepper and toss well. Refrigerate for at least 30 minutes, but not more than an hour. Toss again before serving.

I grew up eating Corky's Barbecue from the time that I was very little until I moved away. I just recently got to go back to Corky's for the first time in more than 11 years, and it was just as good as I remembered! People west of the Mississippi don't seem to know how to make pork barbecue. Corky's does.

— Holly Brumfield,
long-time fan of Corky's

APPLE COLESLAW

The apple adds sweetness and crunch, complementing the flavors of a classic vinaigrette. You can prepare the vinaigrette, veggies, and apples ahead of time, and assemble at the last minute. To keep the apples fresh, store in cold water mixed with lemon juice.

YIELDS: 8 servings
CORKY'S FAMILY: Sarah Duffala

¼ cup apple cider vinegar

2 tablespoons Dijon mustard

2 tablespoons honey

1 tablespoon sugar

¾ teaspoon salt

¼ teaspoon freshly ground black pepper

¼ cup canola oil

1 (16-ounce) package coleslaw mix

4 green onions, sliced (*scant ½ cup*)

2 ribs celery, diced

1 to 2 small Honeycrisp, Gala, or Pink Lady apples, cored and chopped

In a small bowl, whisk together the vinegar, mustard, honey, sugar, salt, and pepper. Gradually add the oil in a slow, steady stream, whisking constantly until emulsified. In a large bowl, combine the coleslaw mix, green onions, celery, and apple. Add the vinegar mixture and toss to coat. Serve immediately.

CAJUN-GOOD COLESLAW

Try this slaw for your next big crowd—it doubles and triples with no problem and adds a bit of zip beyond your ordinary coleslaw. To make ahead, keep the veggies separate from the dressing and toss together at the last minute.

YIELDS: 8 to 10 servings
CORKY'S FRIEND: Lori Hada

½ cup mayonnaise

⅓ cup sugar

¼ cup milk

¼ cup buttermilk

2½ tablespoons freshly squeezed lemon juice (*from about 1 lemon*)

1½ tablespoons white vinegar

½ teaspoon salt

⅛ teaspoon freshly ground black pepper

1 (16-ounce) package coleslaw mix

2 tablespoons minced onion

1 teaspoon Cajun seasoning

To make the dressing, whisk together the mayonnaise, sugar, milk, buttermilk, lemon juice, vinegar, salt, and pepper in a small bowl. In a separate bowl, combine the coleslaw mix and onion. Add the dressing and Cajun seasoning and toss well. Refrigerate the slaw for 30 minutes before serving.

Apple Cole Slaw

123

Asian Almond Slaw

ASIAN ALMOND SLAW

This crunchy side makes a perfect accompaniment to yummy-sticky spareribs. Season them with Chinese five-spice powder, hoisin, soy sauce, and sherry.

YIELDS: 10 servings
CORKY'S FAMILY: Dona Watts

½ to ¾ cup vegetable oil

½ cup sugar

⅓ cup white vinegar

2 (3-ounce) packages chicken-flavored ramen noodles

2 (16-ounce) packages coleslaw mix

1 cup shelled sunflower seeds

1 bunch green onions, chopped
(about ¾ cup)

1 cup slivered or sliced almonds

To make the dressing, whisk together the oil, sugar, vinegar, and the flavoring packets from the ramen noodles in a small bowl and stir until the sugar is dissolved. The dressing can be made in advance and stored in the refrigerator.

Just before serving, combine the coleslaw mix, sunflower seeds, green onions, and almonds in a large bowl. Crush the ramen noodles over top. Pour the dressing over all and toss well.

BUTTERMILK COLESLAW

This classic Southern-style slaw with buttermilk and celery seed works perfectly atop a pulled-pork sandwich. Use a food processor for finely sliced cabbage.

YIELDS: 6 servings
CORKY'S FRIEND: Holly Brumfield

½ cup mayonnaise

2 tablespoons brown sugar

2 tablespoons apple cider vinegar

2 tablespoons buttermilk

1½ tablespoons Dijon mustard

1 teaspoon kosher salt

1 teaspoon freshly ground black pepper

½ teaspoon celery salt

8 cups finely shredded green cabbage
(from 1 head)

2 cups grated carrots
(from about 6 to 8 medium carrots)

Whisk together the mayonnaise, brown sugar, vinegar, buttermilk, mustard, kosher salt, pepper, and celery salt in a large bowl. Add the cabbage and carrots and toss to combine. Cover and chill until serving time.

SPINACH COLESLAW

Colorful cabbages and onions mix with spinach leaves and zippy mustard for a delicious topping for any sandwich, from turkey to barbecue.

YIELDS: 8 to 10 servings
CORKY'S FAMILY: Sheila Thomas

4 cups shredded green cabbage *(from about ½ head)*

4 cups shredded red cabbage *(from about ½ head)*

3 cups sliced fresh spinach *(about 8 ounces)*

1 medium-size red onion, thinly sliced

1 bunch green onions, chopped *(about ¾ cup)*

½ cup chopped parsley

1 cup mayonnaise

¼ cup spicy mustard

Salt and freshly ground black pepper *(to taste)*

Mix the cabbages, spinach, onions, and parsley together in a large bowl. To make the dressing, combine the mayonnaise and mustard and stir well. Add the dressing to the vegetables and toss gently. Season to taste with salt and pepper. Cover and refrigerate for at least an hour before serving.

NOT YOUR MOM'S COLESLAW

Carrots, broccoli, and lemon zest give a fresh twist on the usual.

YIELDS: 14 to 16 servings
CORKY'S FRIEND: Sharon Cook

1 cup mayonnaise

½ cup milk

3 tablespoons lemon zest *(from about 3 medium lemons)*

½ cup freshly squeezed lemon juice *(from about 2 to 3 medium lemons)*, **divided**

1 tablespoon sugar

1 (10-ounce) package shredded carrots

2 (16-ounce) packages broccoli slaw mix

1 (16-ounce) package coleslaw mix

4 medium shallots, finely diced *(about 1 cup)*

2 teaspoons sea salt

2 tablespoons freshly ground black pepper

To make the dressing, whisk together the mayonnaise, milk, ¼ cup of the lemon juice, lemon zest, and sugar in a medium bowl.

In a small bowl, combine the carrots with the remaining ¼ cup lemon juice. Refrigerate until ready to use.

Just before serving, combine the carrots with the broccoli slaw, coleslaw, and shallots in a large bowl. Pour the dressing over the slaw mixture and toss to coat. Season to taste with salt and pepper.

Spinach Coleslaw

THIRTY DAY VINEGAR SLAW

This go-to vinegar slaw will keep for weeks in the fridge—30 days, it's true!—and makes a perfect condiment for shredded meats.

YIELDS: 8 servings

CORKY'S FAMILY: Lew Bilbrey

1 head cabbage, shredded

1 large bell pepper, chopped

1 large onion, chopped
(about 2 cups)

1 cup sugar

1 cup white vinegar

1 teaspoon salt

1 teaspoon mustard seed

1 teaspoon celery seed

½ teaspoon ground turmeric

In a large bowl, combine the cabbage, bell pepper, and onion, tossing to mix well.

Place the sugar, vinegar, salt, mustard seed, celery seed, and turmeric in a saucepan over medium heat. Bring the mixture to a boil, stirring occasionally, until the sugar dissolves. Remove from the heat and carefully pour the hot mixture over the vegetables. Toss to coat.

This slaw can be stored in the refrigerator for up to 30 days.

Corky's . . . it's like a family. It brings generations of people together. I've worked here for over 15 years and now my son works here, too. Our employees stick around, and that brings consistency to Corky's. We have fun, too.

— *Lew Bilbrey, manager of Corky's Collierville*

How do you describe heavenly bliss? **Four words: Corky's Dry Rub Ribs.** *The meat is so tender and tasty after being smoked for hours that it falls right off the bone. If I were a pig, I would be honored to be slaughtered and served up on a plate at Corky's. I've tried BBQ all over the country and nothing even comes close to Corky's ribs. They don't go wrong on much: the barbecue beans are delicious and sweet,* **the cole slaw unbelievable,** *and the buttered rolls are to die for. Plus, they have the Southern requisite beverage: sweet tea.* **The pulled pork is excellent** *as well, but I go to Corky's for the ribs. The service is fast and attentive, once you've actually been seated. The parking can be difficult and the wait can be long during peak hours, but it's worth it. I highly recommend the original location on Poplar. It just tastes better to me. Without a doubt,* **Corky's is the #1 thing I miss about Memphis!** *(Except for my parents.) Also, they FedEx ribs if you don't live in Memphis. Worry about the coronary later. When you go to Corky's, you need to indulge.*

— a review from Andrew, San Francisco, CA

BEANS

Mona's Easy
Baked Beans

CLASSIC MEMPHIS BAKED BEANS

"As a Memphian living in Texas, I'm served way more brisket than any girl should have to deal with," says Martha. "So for my 40th birthday, I decided to celebrate with a major spread of Memphis-style 'cue and made all my favorite Southern sides—mac & cheese, butter beans, biscuits, and those BBQ must-haves, beans and slaw. Here are the beans I baked that night."

YIELDS: 8 to 10 servings

CORKY'S FRIEND: Martha Hopkins

1 medium onion, chopped

1 medium bell pepper, seeded and chopped

½ tablespoon olive oil

1 (28-ounce) can pork and beans

1 cup Corky's Original Recipe Bar-B-Q Sauce

¼ cup packed brown sugar

2 tablespoons molasses

2 cloves garlic, minced

¾ teaspoon ground mustard

½ teaspoon ground red pepper

Preheat the oven to 350°F. In a medium pan over medium heat, sauté the onion and bell pepper in oil until tender. In a large, oven-safe casserole dish, combine the beans and the remaining ingredients. Stir in the onion and bell pepper. Bake, uncovered, until bubbly and warmed throughout, about 45 minutes.

MONA'S EASY BAKED BEANS

YIELDS: 8 servings

CORKY'S FAMILY: Mona Ashcraft

2 (16-ounce) cans pork and beans

½ cup chopped onion
(about ½ small onion)

2 tablespoons brown sugar

1 tablespoon Worcestershire sauce

1 teaspoon yellow mustard

4 slices uncooked bacon

Preheat the oven to 350°F. In a large bowl, combine all the ingredients except the bacon. Pour the mixture into a 1½ quart casserole dish and arrange the bacon slices on top. (For an exceptionally attractive dish, arrange the bacon in a latticework pattern.) Bake, uncovered, until the beans are bubbling, the flavors have melded, and the bacon is cooked, about 45 minutes.

BLACK DOG'S BEER BAKED BEANS

This recipe comes to us courtesy of Corky's manager Keith "Black Dog" Fisher. The ground beef makes it a one-dish meal that cooks up quickly for a weeknight dinner or a football get-together.

YIELDS: 10 to 12 servings

CORKY'S FAMILY: Keith Fisher

1½ pounds ground beef

1 cup chopped onion (from about 1 small onion)

2 (28-ounce) cans baked beans (Bush's Original preferred)

1 cup packed brown sugar

½ cup yellow mustard

1 (18-ounce) bottle Corky's Bar-B-Q Sauce (Original Recipe, Smokin' Hot, or Apple)

12 ounces beer

Brown the ground beef in a medium, nonstick skillet over medium-high heat. Add the onion and cook until it begins to soften, about 1 minute. Remove from the heat and drain the excess fat. Transfer the beef and onion mixture to a 2-quart saucepan, and add the remaining ingredients. Bring to a boil over medium-high heat, reduce the heat to low, and simmer for 30 minutes.

I love you Corky's!!!! I order your ribs online and have them shipped to me in Virginia. But it's not the same, because I need your pulled pork and nachos to accompany my ribs. Every time I'm in Memphis I make it a point to eat here. I must confess, though, the last time I was in Memphis I didn't visit. Boy, was I upset. Instead I tried this place called [deleted competitor's name]. BIG MISTAKE! I felt like such a traitor! I will never do you wrong again, Corky's, and promise when I'm back in December, you'll be the first place I visit.

— a review from Stephanie, Virginia Beach, VA

BEANS WITH A KICK

The variety of beans used in this recipe provides a more complex dish than typical baked beans. For a bolder flavor, substitute Corky's Smokin' Hot Bar-B-Q Sauce.

YIELDS: 12 servings

CORKY'S FRIEND: Ginger Smith

1 pound mild sausage or ground beef

1 small onion, chopped *(about 1 cup)*

1 small bell pepper, seeded and chopped

2 (28-ounce) cans seasoned pinto beans *(Ranch Style beans preferred)*

3 cups Corky's Original Recipe Bar-B-Q Sauce *(from two 18-ounce bottles)*

1 (15-ounce) can black beans, drained and rinsed

1 (15-ounce) can kidney beans, drained and rinsed

1 (10-ounce) can diced tomatoes and green chilies *(mild Ro*Tel preferred)*

¾ cup firmly packed light brown sugar

¼ cup yellow mustard

1 teaspoon freshly ground black pepper

1 teaspoon garlic powder

1 teaspoon Worcestershire sauce

½ teaspoon red pepper

Preheat the oven to 350°F. In a medium sauté pan, brown the sausage or ground beef over medium-high heat; using a slotted spoon, transfer meat to large bowl. Pour off all but 1 tablespoon drippings from the sauté pan. Return the sauté pan to medium heat and add the onion and bell pepper. Sauté until softened, and then add to the meat in the bowl. Add the remaining ingredients, using a rubber spatula to gently combine. Transfer to a 13 x 9-inch casserole dish. Bake until warm and bubbly, about 30 minutes.

CALICO BAR-B-Q BEANS

These beans make for a great side dish, but can easily become a main course with the simple addition of sliced smoked sausage or browned ground beef. Leftovers—if you're lucky enough to have any—can be stored in an airtight container and frozen for up to 3 months.

YIELDS: 10 servings

CORKY'S FRIEND: Sharon Cook

2 (16-ounce) cans baked beans

1 (18-ounce) bottle Corky's Original Recipe Bar-B-Q Sauce

1 (15-ounce) can kidney beans, drained and rinsed

1 (15-ounce) can black beans, drained and rinsed

1 (15-ounce) can giant butter or lima beans, drained and rinsed

1 (12-ounce) jar roasted red pepper strips

1 large sweet onion, chopped (about 2 cups)

½ cup ketchup

½ cup yellow mustard

8 slices fully cooked bacon, cut in half

Preheat the oven to 350°F. Combine all the ingredients except the bacon in a large roasting pan and mix thoroughly. Cook, covered, 1 hour. Remove the roasting pan from the oven, and arrange the bacon strips in a pleasing pattern on top. Reduce the oven heat to 175°F and cook, covered, an additional 30 minutes. Keep warm until ready to serve.

When my brother, Barry, and I were 8 or 9, we'd take the bus from Kirby Parkway and Poplar to Dad's first restaurant, the Public Eye in Overton Square. We loved it there, with the ice-skating rink and a candy store. At the restaurant, we'd sit at his desk and take orders. Our dad was a workaholic, but he always had dinner with us at 5 pm every day.

— *Tricia Woodman, daughter of Corky's founder*

High Country Baked Beans

Black Dog's Beer Baked Beans

Beans with a Kick

Calico Bar-B-Q Beans

Mona's Easy Baked Beans

HIGH COUNTRY BAKED BEANS

According to customer John DuPriest, "When I talk about BBQ with friends and family, I frequently comment that BBQ should be considered one of mankind's highest art forms—and certainly one of its oldest! Sometimes all I get back is a blank stare. But other times, the lucky elected return nods of knowing agreement. Good BBQ—great BBQ—is an occasion of seductive aromas, work followed by leisure, a combination of family and friends, and the spotlight meats holding hands with captivating side dishes. A good side of baked beans is pretty much indispensable to a great BBQ get together. This recipe is simple and delicious. You'll love it."

YIELDS: 6 servings

CORKY'S FRIEND: John DuPriest

3 slices uncooked bacon, diced

1 medium onion, chopped
(about 1½ cups)

¼ cup Tennessee sour mash
whiskey (such as Jack Daniels)

2 (16-ounce) cans baked beans
(Bush's Original preferred)

¼ cup molasses or
dark brown sugar

2 tablespoons ketchup

2 tablespoons Corky's Original
Recipe Bar-B-Q Sauce

1½ tablespoons yellow mustard

In a large Dutch oven over medium heat, sauté the bacon until the fat begins to render. Remove the bacon from the pan and reserve for garnish. Pour off all but 1 tablespoon of the bacon fat and add the onion. Cook until the onion starts to brown around the edges, about 5 minutes. Carefully add the whiskey and continue cooking until the liquid is reduced by half.

Add the beans to the Dutch oven and follow with all of the remaining ingredients. Stir gently until the ingredients are blended. Reduce the heat to low, partially cover, and simmer until heated through, about 5 to 10 minutes (or bake, uncovered, in a 325°F oven for 15 to 20 minutes). Take care not to overcook as the beans will begin to break down. Top with the reserved bacon.

Serve with Bar-B-Q ribs, slices of white bread, and coleslaw for some good eatin'!

My wife Sherry and I live along the foothills of Colorado's Rocky Mountains. When the urge strikes, we have been known to drive the 1000 miles or more to Memphis for its fantastic BBQ. Corky's is our favorite. The drive makes for a fun road trip on America's byways, with good conversation about BBQ filling the time both ways.
— John DuPriest

MISS TOOTIE'S BAR-B-Q BEANS

This recipe can easily be doubled or tripled, and you can use your favorite brand of beans for the base. For a spicier dish, use a combination of Corky's Smokin' Hot Bar-B-Q Sauce and Corky's Original Recipe Bar-B-Q Sauce.

YIELDS: 20 to 24 servings

CORKY'S FRIEND: Tootie Patrick

1 pound bacon, chopped

1 large onion, chopped *(about 2 cups)*

⅔ cup ketchup

⅔ cup Corky's Original Recipe Bar-B-Q Sauce

¼ cup Dijon mustard

¼ cup plus 1 tablespoon molasses

1¼ teaspoons chili powder

¾ teaspoon salt

1 teaspoon freshly ground black pepper

2 (15-ounce) cans black beans, drained and rinsed

2 (15-ounce) cans red kidney beans, drained and rinsed

2 (15-ounce) cans butter beans, drained and rinsed

2 (15-ounce) cans pork and beans, drained

Preheat the oven to 350°F. Place a large, oven-safe pot over medium high heat. Add the bacon and onion and cook until the bacon fat has begun to render and the onion has begun to brown, about 5 to 7 minutes. Drain the excess fat.

Add the ketchup, Bar-B-Q Sauce, molasses, mustard, chili powder, salt, and pepper to the pot and stir to combine. Add the beans and mix gently but well. Transfer the pot to the oven and bake, covered, for 1 hour.

Throughout the 1990s my husband, Chuck, traveled the US to visit his sales reps. One of the reps lived in Memphis and took Chuck to eat at his favorite BBQ place: Corky's. It quickly became my husband's favorite BBQ as well, and he brought home a bottle of Corky's BBQ sauce. I tried it in my bean recipe—delicious! From then on, each time his sales rep visited us in California, he brought us more Corky's BBQ sauce. He would also send us ribs packed in dry ice. Years have passed, and we still order the sauce online. It's a must for my beans, and for my son's baseball team dinners!

—Tootie

Francis Brown's
Layered Mac N' Cheese

Grilled Okra

Grilled Veggie
Kabobs
with Herb
Vinaigrette
Marinade

Jimmy's Bacon-Grilled
Corn on the Cob

TRIMMINGS

LOOKING FOR A VERITABLE SIDEBOARD OF **SIDE DISHES**? YOU HAVE COME TO THE RIGHT CHAPTER! "TRIMMINGS" AS WE CALL THEM IN THE SOUTH ARE ALL THE DISHES *SUPPORTING* THE MAIN COURSE. THEY'RE THE "ORNAMENTS TO YOUR CHRISTMAS TREE, THE HUSH PUPPIES TO YOUR CATFISH, THE SQUASH CASSEROLE TO YOUR SPIRAL-CUT HAM, THE MAC AND **CHEESE** TO YOUR RIB EYE.

CORKY'S SEASONED GREEN BEAN BUNDLES

These bundles are a great make-ahead dish for a large dinner party or for a Thanksgiving meal. You can prepare one to two bundles per guest, assemble the whole thing the day before (or freeze a few weeks ahead), and pop it into the oven just before dinnertime. The green bean bundles can also be grilled over medium heat. Place on the grill and watch carefully, as bacon grease can cause flare-ups, or wrap in foil. They're ready when the bacon is done. Note that you will need toothpicks for this recipe.

YIELDS: 8 servings

CORKY'S FRIEND: Angela Rutland

1 teaspoon Corky's Bar-B-Q Dry Rub, divided

2 pounds fresh green beans, washed and ends trimmed, or 2 (14.5-ounce) cans whole green beans

8 slices bacon, cut in half crosswise

¼ teaspoon garlic salt

¼ cup (½ stick) unsalted butter, melted

3 tablespoons packed brown sugar

Preheat the oven to 350°F. If using fresh beans, bring a pot of water with ½ teaspoon dry rub to a boil; add the beans and cook until crisp-tender, about 6 to 8 minutes. Drain and let cool until cool enough to handle.

Bundle approximately 6 freshly blanched or canned beans together, wrap with a half slice of bacon, and secure with a toothpick. Place the bundles in a 13 x 9-inch baking dish. (Can be prepared ahead of time. Refrigerate or freeze the bundles until ready to use.)

Sprinkle the bundles with garlic salt and remaining ½ teaspoon dry rub. Pour the melted butter over the bundles and then sprinkle with brown sugar. Bake until the bacon is done and the beans are warm, about 15 to 20 minutes.

Soak the skewers to infuse them with flavor.

GRILLED VEGGIE KABOBS WITH HERB VINAIGRETTE MARINADE

YIELDS: 6 to 8 servings

CORKY'S FAMILY: Sheila Thomas

Marinade

½ cup olive oil

¼ cup red wine vinegar

1 garlic clove, minced

1 teaspoon chopped fresh rosemary

1 teaspoon chopped fresh basil

1 teaspoon fresh thyme leaves

1 teaspoon chopped fresh oregano

½ teaspoon sea salt

½ teaspoon freshly ground black pepper

Kabobs

2 large red onions, cut into 1½-inch pieces

2 medium-size red, yellow, or orange bell peppers, cut into 1½-inch pieces

2 medium zucchini, cut crosswise into ¾-inch slices

2 medium-size yellow summer squash, cut crosswise into ¾-inch slices

1 (8-ounce) package small fresh mushrooms *(button or crimini)*

1 pint cherry tomatoes

1 medium-size green bell pepper, cut into 1½-inch pieces

For marinade: Combine all the ingredients in a small bowl and whisk to blend.

For kabobs: Thread all of the vegetables onto skewers, alternating colors, textures, and flavors. If using bamboo skewers, wrap the ends in foil to prevent burning.

Place the finished kabobs in a 13 x 9-inch baking dish. Pour the marinade over the kabobs, turning to coat. Cover and chill for at least 2 hours.

Prepare a grill for medium-heat cooking. Remove the kabobs from the marinade, reserving the marinade. Grill the kabobs until tender, basting with the reserved marinade, about 10 to 12 minutes. Serve the kabobs warm or at room temperature, on or off the skewer.

My favorite Corky's memory is taking my kids there for the first time and watching them try the ribs. My younger daughter loves them to this day, though we don't have access to good ribs now that we've moved. We order the dry rub, though, and the kids use it on everything.

— Ray Woodward, long-time fan of Corky's

AUNT RUTHIE'S SWEET POTATO CASSEROLE

"Come Thanksgiving my family gets demanding, especially when it comes to sweet potato casseroles," says Lucy. "If I even think of switching to roasted yams, heaven forbid, or a fluffy marshmallow-topped dish, there is an uprising. For us, the praline-like topping reminds us that, indeed, we have much to be thankful for."

YIELDS: 8 servings

CORKY'S FAMILY: Lucy Stovall

Sweet Potatoes

4 cups cooked, mashed sweet potatoes *(from about 3 pounds potatoes)*

½ cup sugar

2 large eggs

⅓ cup milk

¼ cup (½ stick) unsalted butter or margarine, melted

1 teaspoon vanilla extract

Nonstick cooking spray, oil, or butter

Topping

⅔ cup lightly packed brown sugar

½ cup finely chopped pecans

⅓ cup all-purpose flour

⅓ cup (5 tablespoons plus 1 teaspoon) unsalted butter or margarine

For sweet potatoes: Preheat the oven to 350°F. Using nonstick spray, oil, or butter, grease a 2-quart baking dish. Combine the sweet potatoes, sugar, eggs, milk, butter, and vanilla in a large bowl. Using an electric mixer, beat until smooth. Spoon into the prepared dish.

For topping: Combine all the ingredients in a medium bowl and mix well. Sprinkle over the casserole. Bake, uncovered, until the potatoes are warm throughout and the topping is golden brown, about 30 minutes.

GRILLED ASPARAGUS

Little tastes better than freshly grilled veggies. Choose fatter asparagus spears for the grill, as they'll hold up to the fire better than thinner ones.

YIELDS: 6 servings
CORKY'S FRIEND: Douglas Corder

2 bunches (about 2 pounds) fresh asparagus, tough ends trimmed

2 tablespoons olive oil

1 teaspoon Corky's Bar-B-Q Dry Rub

Sea salt and freshly ground black pepper *(to taste)*

Prepare a grill for medium-heat cooking. Lay the asparagus out on a platter and drizzle with the olive oil. Sprinkle with dry rub; season to taste with salt and pepper. Toss to coat evenly.

Place the asparagus spears directly onto the grill, crosswise to the grates so that the spears won't fall through. Grill until crisp-tender, turning as needed, about 5 to 10 minutes.

SOUTHERN BUTTER BEANS

YIELDS: 6 to 8 servings
CORKY'S FAMILY: Carol Sweeney

1 small onion, minced *(about 1 cup)*

5 slices bacon, diced

½ cup firmly packed brown sugar

1 (16-ounce) package frozen butter beans

¼ cup (½ stick) unsalted butter

2 teaspoons salt

1 teaspoon freshly ground black pepper

Cook the onion and bacon in a large Dutch oven set over medium heat for 5 to 7 minutes. Add the brown sugar and cook, stirring occasionally, until the sugar is melted, about 1 to 2 minutes. Add the butter beans and butter and stir until the butter is melted and the beans are thoroughly coated.

Pour enough water to come 1 to 2 inches above the beans. Increase the heat to medium high, and bring the beans to a boil. Reduce the heat to low and simmer, stirring occasionally, for 2 hours or until the beans are very tender and the liquid has thickened and comes just below the level of the beans. (Add more water if needed during cooking.) Season with salt and freshly ground black pepper.

JIMMY'S BACON-GRILLED CORN ON THE COB

YIELDS: 8 servings

CORKY'S FAMILY: Jimmy Stovall

½ cup (1 stick) unsalted butter, melted

1 teaspoon Corky's Bar-B-Q Dry Rub

8 ears corn on the cob

8 slices applewood-smoked bacon

Prepare a grill for medium-heat cooking. In a small bowl, mix together the melted butter and dry rub. Pull back the corn husks, leaving them attached, and remove all silk. Brush each ear with the butter mixture and wrap with a slice of bacon. (Or, for a vegetarian option, sprinkle the corn with Parmesan cheese and season with black pepper and minced parsley instead.) Replace the husk around the corn and wrap with foil. Grill, turning once, until the bacon is cooked, about 20 to 25 minutes.

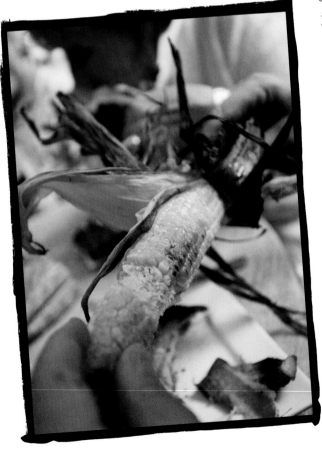

Nom, nom, nom!

Don't forget the rub!

COUSIN KATIE'S SPINACH CASSEROLE

Jimmy's cousin Katie is known for her famous spinach casserole and is now expected to bring it to every family holiday gathering. Katie, who is also a member of the Corky's work family, has been with us since her sweet 16. We won't go into just how many years that is. Let's just say she's a keeper!

YIELDS: 6 to 8 servings

CORKY'S FAMILY: Katie Witham

Nonstick cooking spray, oil, or butter

3 (16-ounce bags) frozen spinach

¼ cup minced garlic *(from about 12 garlic cloves)*

2 (0.7-ounce) packages Italian salad dressing mix

2 (8-ounce packages) cream cheese, softened

1 medium-size white onion, diced *(about 1½ cups)*

2 cups (8 ounces) shredded sharp Cheddar cheese

Preheat the oven to 350°F. Using the nonstick cooking spray, oil, or butter, grease a 13 x 9-inch baking dish. Cook the spinach on the stovetop according to the package directions, mixing in the garlic and Italian salad dressing mix. Drain the mixture and transfer to the prepared pan. In a medium bowl, combine the cream cheese and onion; smooth mixture over the spinach. Top with the Cheddar cheese and bake until bubbly and warmed throughout, about 20 to 30 minutes.

So yummy even the kids will love it!

LAUREN'S MEGA MAC AND CHEESE WITH BACON

If you have leftover pulled pork, add a layer to the mac and cheese. Serve with a fresh green salad for a lovely meal.

YIELDS: 8 to 10 servings

CORKY'S FRIEND: Lauren Edmonds

Topping

1 cup panko bread crumbs

2 tablespoons (¼ stick) unsalted butter, melted

1 tablespoon finely chopped parsley

½ teaspoon kosher or sea salt

Mac and Cheese

6 slices thick-cut applewood-smoked bacon

1 pound cavatappi pasta *(spiral macaroni)*

3 cups whole milk

¾ cup heavy whipping cream

¼ cup (½ stick) unsalted butter

¼ cup all-purpose flour

1 teaspoon ground mustard

¾ teaspoon kosher or sea salt

½ teaspoon freshly ground black pepper

½ teaspoon onion powder

8 ounces (2 cups) shredded Gruyère cheese

8 ounces (2 cups) shredded white Cheddar cheese

For topping: Combine all the ingredients in a small bowl. Set aside.

For mac and cheese: Preheat the oven to 350°F. Cook the bacon in a pan set over medium-high heat until the fat is rendered. Transfer the bacon to a paper-towel-lined plate to drain. Reserve 1 tablespoon of the bacon grease from the pan. When the bacon is cool, crumble coarsely.

Bring a large pot of salted water to a boil; add the pasta and cook until al dente. Drain well.

Heat the milk and cream in a saucepan over medium heat until hot, taking care not to boil. In a large pot over medium-low heat, melt the butter and reserved bacon grease. Whisk in the flour and cook until the flour is completely incorporated and turning golden, about 2 minutes. Slowly add the hot milk and cream, whisking until smooth. Cook until bubbly and thickened, about 1 to 2 minutes longer. Mix in the mustard, salt, pepper, and onion powder. Remove from the heat. Add the cheeses, stirring occasionally, until melted completely. Add the bacon and the cooked pasta and stir well. Pour the mixture into a 3-quart baking dish or a 13 x 9-inch casserole dish and top with the topping mixture. Bake in the center of the oven until golden brown, about 20 minutes.

Try adding leftover pork for a delicious twist.

FRANCES BROWN'S LAYERED MAC N' CHEESE

This down-home mac goes beyond the expected Cheddar and Velveeta, with layers of Colby Jack between the noodles for extra cheesy goodness.

YIELDS: 6 servings

CORKY'S FAMILY: Gwen Barr

8 ounces (about 2 cups) elbow macaroni

Nonstick cooking spray, oil, or butter

2 cups milk

2 tablespoons (¼ stick) unsalted butter

1 tablespoon mustard

¼ cup all-purpose flour

8 ounces processed cheese, cubed

1 cup (4 ounces) shredded Cheddar cheese

8 slices Colby Jack cheese

Bring a large pot of salted water to a boil; add the macaroni and cook until al dente. Drain and return to the pot. Preheat the oven to 350°F. Using the nonstick spray, oil, or butter, grease a 2-quart casserole dish. In a medium saucepan over medium heat, bring the milk, butter, and mustard to a simmer. Whisk in the flour. Continue to cook, stirring constantly to prevent burning, until the mixture is thick and bubbly, about 5 to 7 minutes. Reduce the heat, add the processed cheese, and stir until completely melted. Pour the cheese sauce and shredded Cheddar cheese over the cooked pasta in the pot, stirring to evenly coat.

Transfer half of the pasta mixture to the prepared casserole dish. Top with an even layer of the Colby Jack cheese slices. Top the cheese slices with the remaining pasta mixture. Bake, uncovered, until the top is golden brown, about 30 minutes. Let stand 10 minutes before serving.

GRILLED OKRA

Many Southerners won't venture beyond fried okra, and that's a shame. Okra has an unfair reputation for being slimy, which keeps many people from realizing just how wonderful this flavorful, versatile vegetable can taste. The next time you see these colorful little pods at the grocery store or farmers' market, give them a try. You won't believe how fresh and yummy they taste—with no slime in sight!

YIELDS: 4 servings

CORKY'S FAMILY: Sheila Thomas

1 pound small okra pods

¼ cup olive oil

2 garlic cloves, minced

Salt and freshly ground black pepper (to taste)

Prepare a grill for medium-high heat cooking. Wash the okra and pat dry. In a small bowl combine the olive oil and garlic; add salt and pepper to taste. Thread the okra pods onto two skewers, alternating the direction of the caps for even cooking. Place the skewers on a plate or shallow dish and pour the olive oil mixture over them, turning for even coating.

Grill until grill marks show but the okra is still crisp, turning once, about 4 to 5 minutes per side. Transfer to a serving platter and serve either on or off the skewers. Both the Chipotle Mayonnaise (page 34) and Bar-B-Q Ranch Dipping Sauce and Dressing (page 33) are nice served with this easy appetizer, but the okra tastes equally delicious all on its own.

WATERSHED OKRA FRITTERS

We're partial to frying okra in this batter, but many fresh vegetables, from chopped cauliflower to diced squash, would work in the fritters here. Serve with Chipotle Mayonnaise (page 34) as the dipping sauce.

YIELDS: 6 to 8 servings

CORKY'S FAMILY: Geneva Smith

½ cup white cornmeal

½ cup all-purpose flour

2 teaspoons salt, divided

1 teaspoon baking powder

1 medium egg, lightly beaten

½ cup water

½ medium onion, finely chopped *(about ¾ cup)*

2 cups thinly sliced okra

½ teaspoon freshly ground black pepper

Canola oil *(for frying)*

Combine the cornmeal, flour, 1½ teaspoons salt, and baking powder in a mixing bowl. In a separate bowl, whisk together the egg and ½ cup of water. Add to the dry ingredients and mix until moist. Combine the onion and okra in a large bowl and sprinkle with the remaining ½ teaspoon salt and pepper; toss lightly. Fold the vegetables into the batter.

Pour enough oil to reach a depth of 1 inch in a heavy skillet. Heat over medium-high heat until the oil reaches 340°F. Carefully spoon the okra batter by heaping tablespoons into the hot oil, taking care not to overcrowd the pan. Fry until the fritters are golden brown on one side, then carefully flip and continue frying until both sides are browned. Remove the fritters from the skillet and drain on paper towels. Serve immediately.

SQUASH PUPPIES

This is a fun twist on hush puppies that replaces most of the cornmeal with summer squash. It works equally well as an appetizer or a side dish to any Southern meal.

YIELDS: 4 to 6 servings

CORKY'S FRIEND: Leigh Ann Wills

5 to 6 small summer squash, diced and cooked (about 2 cups)

¼ cup finely chopped onion (from about ¼ small onion)

1 medium egg

2 tablespoons sugar

2 tablespoons (¼ stick) unsalted butter, melted

Salt and freshly ground black pepper (to taste)

½ cup self-rising flour

½ cup cornmeal

Vegetable oil (for frying)

In a large bowl, combine the squash and onion. In a small bowl, whisk the egg, sugar, and butter to blend; season with salt and freshly ground pepper. Add the egg mixture to the squash and onion and stir to mix well. In a small bowl, mix together the flour and cornmeal. Slowly add the flour and cornmeal mixture to the squash mixture, using a rubber spatula to fold the dry ingredients in. (The batter should be thick enough to hold its form while frying.)

Using a large pot, Dutch oven, or electric fryer, pour in enough oil to reach a depth of 3 to 4 inches; heat over medium-high heat to 350°F. Carefully drop small spoonfuls of the batter into the hot oil. Cook until golden brown, turning once. Using a slotted spoon, transfer the cooked squash puppies to a paper-towel-lined plate to drain. Serve hot.

TRADITIONAL HUSHPUPPIES

YIELDS: 6 servings

CORKY'S FAMILY: Carol Sweeney

1½ cups milk

¾ cup sugar

2 large eggs

2 tablespoons salt

1 tablespoon baking powder

1½ teaspoons garlic powder

1½ teaspoons freshly ground black pepper

1 cup chopped onion *(from about 1 small onion)*

¼ cup chopped jalapeño peppers *(from about 2 to 3 jalapeño peppers)*

2 cups self-rising flour

2 cups yellow cornmeal

Oil *(for frying)*

In a large bowl, combine the milk, sugar, eggs, salt, baking powder, garlic powder, and pepper, whisking to blend well (bubbles will appear). Stir in the onion and jalapeños. Slowly add the flour and the cornmeal, stirring together thoroughly. The batter should be the consistency of cookie dough.

Using a large pot, Dutch oven, or electric fryer, pour in enough oil to reach a depth of 3 to 4 inches; heat over medium-high heat to 350°F. Using a small scoop or tablespoon, carefully drop balls of the batter into the oil and cook, turning once, until golden and cooked through, about 4 minutes. Using a slotted spoon, transfer the hushpuppies to a paper-towel-lined plate to drain. Serve hot.

HOW CORKY'S GOT ITS NAME

Don Pelts was a fan of the 1982 film Porky's. *(This is not a judgment call; it's merely the facts.) He loved it so much, that he decided it would be the perfect name for his new barbecue restaurant. Perfect, that is, until he received a cease-and-desist letter. But Don is nothing if not flexible. He switched that P for a C and opened the landmark restaurant we know and love today.*

MAMA STELLA'S TURNIP GREENS

This recipe comes courtesy of Gwen Barr, passed down from her grandmother, Mama Stella. Gwen started out in the office at Corky's. She has filled many roles during her tenure, including being the leading force behind our Adopt-A-School program with a local elementary school. Gwen would give you the shirt off her back and will help anyone in need. That said, if you are a new employee under Sergeant Barr's training, you might not see this giving side—but if you hang on and follow her rules, you will! If you'd like a more healthful choice than salt pork, smoked turkey will flavor your greens just as deliciously.

YIELDS: 6 to 8 servings

CORKY'S FAMILY: Gwen Barr

4½ pounds turnip greens

1 pound salt pork, rinsed and diced

1½ cups water

1 cup finely chopped onion *(from about 1 small onion)*

1 teaspoon sugar *(optional)*

½ teaspoon freshly ground black pepper

Pinch of crushed red pepper flakes

Remove the tough stems and discolored leaves from the greens. Wash the greens thoroughly and drain well. (Do this several times if needed; nothing's worse than grits in your greens!)

In a large pot or Dutch oven set over medium heat, cook the salt pork until crisp, brown, and tender. Add the greens, 1½ cups of water, onion, sugar (if using), black pepper, and crushed pepper, and bring to a boil. Reduce the heat, cover, and simmer until the greens are tender, about 40 to 45 minutes. Taste and adjust the seasonings. Serve the greens with cornbread and vinegar or hot sauce.

MISS AMY'S LOADED BAKED POTATO CASSEROLE

YIELDS: 10 to 12 servings

CORKY'S FRIEND: Amy Newsom

5 pounds baking potatoes

1 cup (8 ounces) sour cream

1 cup mayonnaise

½ cup onion, chopped *(from about ½ small onion)*

½ cup cooked and chopped bacon *(about ⅓ pound uncooked bacon)*

¼ cup (½ stick) unsalted butter, melted

1 (1-ounce) package ranch salad dressing and seasoning mix

½ cup (4 ounces) shredded Cheddar cheese

Nonstick cooking spray, oil, or butter

Preheat the oven to 400°F. Scrub the potatoes well, rinse under cool running water, and pat dry. Prick the potatoes in several places with a fork and bake until tender, about 1 hour. Remove the potatoes from the oven and place on a wire rack until cool enough to handle. Peel the potatoes and cut the potatoes into chunks.

Reduce the oven heat to 350°F. Using nonstick spray, oil, or butter, grease a 13 x 9-inch baking dish. In a large bowl, mix together the sour cream, mayonnaise, onion, bacon, butter, ranch seasoning mix, and cheese. Add the potatoes and toss gently to combine. Spoon the potato mixture into the prepared dish and bake, uncovered, until hot and bubbly, about 40 to 45 minutes.

159

PEABODY POTATOES

These potatoes are worthy of a place on the menu of the Peabody Hotel. For a real Memphis twist, try a Bar-B-Q version—just before transferring your potatoes to the casserole dish for baking, gently fold in ½ cup of Corky's Original Recipe Bar-B-Q sauce. Serve with Tommy's Bar-B-Q Shrimp (page 194).

YIELDS: 8 to 10 servings

CORKY'S FRIEND: Stephen DiMeglio

6 large russet potatoes

⅔ cup milk

½ cup (1 stick) unsalted butter or margarine, softened

1 (8-ounce) package cream cheese, softened

1 cup (8 ounces) sour cream

¼ cup thinly sliced green onions *(from about 3 green onions)*

1 garlic clove, minced

Salt and freshly ground black pepper *(to taste)*

1 cup (4 ounces) shredded sharp Cheddar cheese

Peel and cube the potatoes. Place the potatoes and a small amount of salted water in a large pot over medium-high heat and bring to a boil. Cook, covered, until the potatoes are tender, about 20 to 25 minutes. Drain and cool slightly.

Preheat the oven to 350°F. Place the cooked potatoes in a large bowl and beat with an electric mixer on low speed. Add the milk and butter and beat until fluffy. Beat in the cream cheese, sour cream, green onions, and garlic. Season to taste with salt and pepper.

Transfer the potato mixture to a 2-quart round casserole dish. Top with the shredded cheese. Bake until the cheese is melted and the potatoes are heated through, about 30 minutes.

NAN'S SQUASH CASSEROLE

YIELDS: 8 to 10 servings

CORKY'S FRIEND: Nan Miller

Nonstick cooking spray, oil, or butter

6 to 8 medium-size yellow squash, sliced into rounds

1 small onion, chopped *(about 1 cup)*

1 chicken bouillon cube

1½ cups grated Parmesan cheese, divided

¾ cup sour cream

¼ cup (½ stick) unsalted butter, melted

2 medium eggs

Salt and freshly ground black pepper *(to taste)*

Preheat the oven to 350°F. Using nonstick spray, oil, or butter, grease a 13 x 9-inch casserole dish. Place the squash, onion, bouillon cube, and enough water to cover the vegetables in a pot over medium heat. Bring to a simmer and cook, covered, until the squash is tender, about 3 to 6 minutes. Remove from the heat and drain well.

Place the cooked squash mixture in a large bowl. Add 1 cup of the Parmesan cheese, sour cream, butter, and eggs and mix well. Season with salt and pepper. Pour the mixture into the prepared dish and top with the remaining ½ cup Parmesan cheese. Bake until bubbling and heated through, about 30 minutes.

I use Corky's regular sauce on their pork shoulder, but their ribs? I don't touch 'em! Since Corky's opened, I've never been able to decide if I preferred the wet or the dry. So I always order the half-and-half. Dadgumit! I've gotten hungry just thinking about these ribs! I'm going to have to get some in the drive-thru.

— *Wes Kraker, life-long Corky's customer, Memphis, TN*

DINNERS

DINNER, SUPPER ~ WHATEVER YOU CALL IT ~ WE SURE LOVED TESTING THESE *family favorites* FOR THE BOOK. MANY OF THEM ARE ≡FAST ENOUGH FOR A WEEKDAY DINNER, BUT GOOD ENOUGH FOR WEEKEND COMPANY. MAKE THE KIDDOS SOME CHICKEN TOMATO PIE, SERVE POPS SOME SWEET APPLE BABY BACK RIBS, AND A healthy SERVING OF QUEEN BEE'S SPAGHETTI GRAVY FOR YOUR WELL-DESERVING SELF!

Brother Al's Southern Fried Chicken

Billie's Dry-Rubbed Rib-Eyes

Tommy's Bar-B-Q Shrimp

Crazy Frase's Bar-B-Q Ribs

Corky's Chicken Enchiladas

CRAZY FRASE'S BAR-B-Q RIBS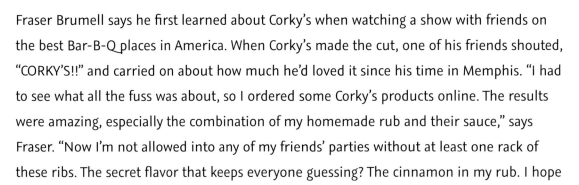

Fraser Brumell says he first learned about Corky's when watching a show with friends on the best Bar-B-Q places in America. When Corky's made the cut, one of his friends shouted, "CORKY'S!!" and carried on about how much he'd loved it since his time in Memphis. "I had to see what all the fuss was about, so I ordered some Corky's products online. The results were amazing, especially the combination of my homemade rub and their sauce," says Fraser. "Now I'm not allowed into any of my friends' parties without at least one rack of these ribs. The secret flavor that keeps everyone guessing? The cinnamon in my rub. I hope you enjoy making, eating, and sharing them as much as I do."

YIELDS: 2 servings per slab

CORKY'S FRIEND: Fraser Brumell

Rub

2 teaspoons seasoned salt

1 teaspoon cayenne pepper

1 teaspoon chili powder

1 teaspoon dry mustard

1 teaspoon ground cinnamon

1 teaspoon sugar

1 teaspoon freshly ground black pepper

1 teaspoon onion powder

Ribs

1 slab baby back ribs

2 cups pineapple juice

1 (12-ounce) can beer

1 (18-ounce) bottle Corky's Original Bar-B-Q Sauce

For rub: Mix all the rub ingredients together in a small bowl.

For ribs: Trim the fat from the ribs and place them in a shallow container. Pour the pineapple juice over the ribs, cover, and refrigerate for 30 minutes.

Pour the juice off of the ribs and pat them down with a paper towel. Sprinkle the rub onto the ribs and rub it in—don't be shy with the rub! Cover and let stand for 10 to 20 minutes in the refrigerator. Prepare a grill for medium-heat cooking. When the coals are ready, push them to one side, fill an aluminum baking pan half-full of beer, and place it under the grill rack. Put the ribs on the grill, meat-side up, as far away from the heat as possible. Rotate the ribs every 45 minutes to allow for even cooking, but do not flip them. Let cook for 1½ to 2½ hours—longer if cooking more than 1 rack. Spread Bar-B-Q sauce on the ribs in the last 20 minutes of cooking and again in the last 10 minutes. Remove from the grill and allow to stand at least 10 minutes before cutting and serving.

SWEET APPLE BABY BACK RIBS 🍖

There's no need to cut these ribs, according to recipe contributor Sharon Rhyne, who says that the meat falls right off the bone. "This cooking method ensures tenderness, and finishing with the Corky's Apple Bar-B-Q sauce ensures perfect flavor," says Sharon. "My son brought me some Corky's rub and sauce after a work stint in Tennessee a few years back. Now Corky's is the only product I'll use for ribs and pulled pork. These ribs are so easy to prepare, they are now one of our weekend favorites!"

YIELDS: 2 servings

CORKY'S FRIEND: Sharon Rhyne

3 pounds baby back ribs

1 (8-ounce) bottle Dijon mustard

1 (2.5-ounce) bottle Corky's Bar-B-Q Dry Rub

1 (18-ounce) bottle Corky's Apple Bar-B-Q Sauce

⅔ cup (or one 5.5-ounce can) apple juice

Remove the membrane from the back of the ribs (or ask your butcher to remove). Place the ribs in a large baking dish or roasting pan. Brush the ribs with mustard on all sides. Unless you're okay with messy, don rubber gloves and add dry rub on all sides of the ribs. Cover the ribs with plastic wrap and refrigerate, allowing the ribs to marinate overnight.

Prepare a smoker for low-heat cooking with mesquite or apple wood, and smoke the ribs for 4 hours.* Preheat the oven to 300°F. Remove the ribs from the grill and place them in a foil-lined pan. Brush the ribs on all sides with the Bar-B-Q sauce and pour the apple juice into the pan. Cover tightly with foil and bake for one hour.

* Don't have a smoker? If using a gas grill for smoking, turn on only one of the burners to the lowest heat possible. Place a foil pouch or pan filled with soaked wood chips directly over the burner and under the grate. Place the meat as far from the heat source as possible and smoke for 4 hours.

THE "CADILLAC" OF BAR-B-Q PORK PIZZA

For a faster meal, use packaged pizza crust or a refrigerated dough. Top the finished pie with frizzled onions or thinly sliced deep-fried onion rings if you're feeling particularly decadent. Don't want to fire up the grill? The pizzas can instead be baked in your oven at 400°F for 10 minutes.

YIELDS: 8 servings

CORKY'S FAMILY: Greg "Cadillac" Harris

Pizza Dough

1 package active dry yeast

1¼ teaspoons sugar, divided

1 cup warm water (105°F-115°F)

¼ cup olive oil, divided

3 cups all purpose flour, plus additional for rolling dough

1 teaspoon salt

½ teaspoon freshly ground black pepper

Nonstick cooking spray, oil, or butter

2 tablespoons cornmeal

Topping

¾ cup prepared pizza sauce

½ cup Corky's Original Recipe Bar-B-Q Sauce

½ pound Corky's Bar-B-Q Pork Shoulder, chopped

1 small red onion, chopped *(about 1 cup)*

1 small green bell pepper, chopped *(about 1 cup)*

1 small red bell pepper, chopped *(about 1 cup)*

2 cups shredded mozzarella

For pizza dough: Sprinkle the yeast and ¼ teaspoon sugar over the warm water in a small bowl and let stand for 10 minutes or until the mixture is bubbly. Stir in 2 tablespoons of the olive oil. In a large bowl, combine the flour, remaining 1 teaspoon sugar, salt, and pepper. Add the yeast mixture to the flour mixture and stir with a wooden spoon to combine (the dough will be sticky).

Turn the dough out onto a lightly floured surface and knead until the dough is smooth and elastic. Using the nonstick spray, oil, or butter, lightly grease a large bowl. Place the dough into the prepared bowl, turning once to grease the surface of the dough. Cover and let rise in a warm place until double in size (45 to 60 minutes), or let rise overnight in the refrigerator.

For topping: While the dough is rising, combine the pizza sauce and barbecue sauce in a small bowl. Prep all the other ingredients for assembling the pizzas.

When the dough has risen, punch it down and then turn onto a lightly floured surface. Cut the dough into 4 equal portions. Cover and let rest for 15 minutes. Pat or roll each portion of dough into an 8-inch circle. For an easy transfer to the grill, place wax paper on a cookie sheet and sprinkle with the cornmeal. Place the dough rounds on the wax paper and brush the tops of the dough with the remaining 2 tablespoons of olive oil.

To assemble the pizzas, prepare a charcoal or gas grill for low-heat cooking and lightly grease the racks. Carefully place 2 of the dough circles, oiled-side down, onto the grill rack, directly over the low coals. Grill for about 6 minutes or until light brown and firm enough to transfer.

Transfer the crust, grilled-side up, to the back of the cookie sheet. Ladle one-fourth of the sauce on the grilled side of each of the crusts and top each with one-fourth of the pork, onion, peppers, and cheese. Carefully transfer the pizzas back to the grill and grill until the crust is crisp and the cheese melts, moving the pizzas as needed to cook evenly. Repeat with the remaining dough and toppings.

GRILLED SWEET APPLE CHOPS

One of Corky's favorite customers discovered pork chop nirvana when she combined Corky's Apple Bar-B-Q Sauce with applesauce and warm spices. The flavors in these pork chops pair beautifully with the Loaded Baked Potato Casserole (page 159).

YIELDS: 4 servings

CORKY'S FRIEND: Paula Uhlrich

1 (18-ounce) bottle Corky's Apple Bar-B-Q Sauce

1 (15-ounce) jar applesauce

½ cup raw sugar *(such as turbinado)*

2 tablespoons ground cinnamon

4 pork chops

In a medium bowl, combine the Bar-B-Q sauce, applesauce, sugar, and cinnamon, adjusting the flavors to your preference. Place the pork chops in a large casserole dish. Pour the sauce over the pork chops, cover with plastic wrap, and refrigerate, allowing the pork to marinate overnight.

Prepare a grill for indirect-heat cooking. Grill the chops over indirect heat until a thermometer registers 145°F, turning once, about 3 to 4 minutes on each side. Remove from the grill and let the chops rest for 10 minutes before serving.

Corky's has been a lifesaver for us. My mom has Alzheimer's and I've been trying to find ways to make things easier for my dad. My mom was always the cook, but now my dad is trying to care for her, take care of home, and get food on the table. Jimmy (from Corky's QVC) heard what was going on and sent a sample of pulled pork and ribs to my parents. They absolutely loved it. It's so easy and good. Honest-to-goodness, down-home comfort food. Now we order meals from Corky's all the time. What a real blessing for my mom and dad.

— Mary Eckenrode, QVC personality and Corky's fan

ASHUNTA'S HONEY-GLAZED PORK TENDERLOIN

The honey-sweet glaze on this tenderloin is a match for Ashunta, a favorite Corky's server whose sweet smile and bubbly personality are a treat for guests and co-workers alike. If you happen to have leftovers (you won't), slice the tenderloin and serve it on hot Sweet Potato Biscuits (page 42) for day-after finger sandwiches.

YIELDS: 4 to 6 servings

CORKY'S FAMILY: Ashunta McCray

½ cup bottled Italian-style vinaigrette

½ cup soy sauce

¼ cup honey

1¾ pounds pork tenderloin, trimmed

Combine the vinaigrette, soy sauce, and honey in a resealable plastic bag and add the pork. Seal the bag and place it in the refrigerator, allowing the pork to marinate several hours or overnight.

Prepare a grill for medium-heat cooking. Remove the pork from the marinade, discarding marinade. Grill the pork, covered, until a meat thermometer registers 145°F, turning once, about 15 to 20 minutes. Let the pork rest for 10 to 15 minutes before slicing.

LITTLE E'S SLOW COOKER BAR-B-Q PORK

Larry Eason has been with Corky's since the doors opened. He started as a busser and is now a manager. He is a hard worker and will work any shift, almost any day of the year. The one exception? Super Bowl Sunday.

YIELDS: 6 servings

CORKY'S FAMILY: Larry Eason

Nonstick cooking spray, oil, or butter

3 to 4 pounds boneless pork shoulder roast (Boston butt), trimmed

1 (18-ounce) bottle Corky's Original Recipe Bar-B-Q Sauce

1 (12-ounce) cola-flavored soft drink

Using the nonstick spray, oil, or butter, lightly grease a 6-quart slow cooker. Place the pork roast in the slow cooker. Pour the Bar-B-Q sauce and cola over the roast. Cover and cook on low until the meat shreds easily with a fork, about 8 to 10 hours. Transfer the pork to a cutting board and shred with two forks, removing any large pieces of fat. Skim the fat from the cooking sauce in the slow cooker. (If time is not an issue, refrigerate the sauce. The fat will rise to the surface and congeal, making it easy to remove. Rewarm the sauce before continuing.) Stir the shredded pork into the warm sauce and serve.

Reggie Cooper, Robbie Levine, and Larry Eason ham for the camera at Corky's first-ever catering job.

SWEET POTATO–PORK SHEPHERD'S PIE

The sweetness of the sweet potatoes makes them a perfect topping for this homey pork.

YIELDS: 6 to 8 servings

CORKY'S FAMILY: Carol Sweeney

4 large sweet potatoes, peeled

1 cup applesauce

2 tablespoons (¼ stick) unsalted butter

2 tablespoons vegetable oil

1 medium onion, chopped *(about 1½ cups)*

2 stalks celery, chopped *(about 1 cup)*

1 pound Corky's Bar-B-Q Pork Shoulder

2 Granny Smith apples, peeled and cubed *(about 2 cups)*

1 cup chicken broth

½ cup apple juice

2 tablespoons minced fresh thyme

1 teaspoon minced fresh sage

Salt and freshly ground black pepper *(to taste)*

2 tablespoons brown sugar

Bring a large pot of salted water to a boil. Add the sweet potatoes and cook until fork-tender, about 30 minutes. Drain and cut into chunks. Return the sweet potatoes to the pot and add the applesauce and butter. Mash together and set aside.

Preheat the oven to 400°F. In a large skillet, heat the oil over medium-high heat. Add the onion and celery and sauté until lightly browned. Add the pork shoulder, apples, broth, apple juice, thyme, sage, and salt and pepper to taste. Reduce the heat and simmer for 5 minutes.

Transfer the pork mixture to a 13 x 9-inch glass baking dish and top with the sweet potato mixture, smoothing out the top. Sprinkle with brown sugar and bake until bubbling on the sides, about 30 minutes.

QUEEN BEE'S SPAGHETTI GRAVY

Robbie Levine, the self-proclaimed Queen Bee of Corky's, has been with Corky's since the early days. While she can cook up some mean Bar-B-Q, one of her family's favorite comfort foods is her Spaghetti Gravy. This traditional Italian marinara sauce tastes outstanding on its own and also makes the perfect base for either Italian meat sauce or Memphis' Famous Bar-B-Q Spaghetti, created right here in Memphis, Tennessee.

YIELDS: 12 servings

CORKY'S FAMILY: Robbie Levine

2 tablespoons olive oil

1 large onion, finely diced
(about 2 cups)

4 garlic cloves, minced

1 pound ground beef or
1 pound ground Italian
sausage or 1 pound Corky's
Bar-B-Q Pork Shoulder plus
½ cup Corky's Original Recipe
Bar-B-Q Sauce

1 (28-ounce) can crushed
tomatoes

1 (15-ounce) can tomato sauce

1 (6-ounce) can tomato paste

2 tablespoons parsley flakes

1 tablespoon dried oregano

1 tablespoon dried basil

2 medium bay leaves

Cooked spaghetti noodles
(for serving)

Heat the oil in a large, heavy-bottomed pot set over medium heat. Add the onion and garlic and sauté until transparent. If making the Traditional Italian Spaghetti variation, add the ground beef or Italian sausage at this stage, cook, and drain off the excess fat. Add the tomatoes, tomato sauce, and tomato paste, stirring well. Add the parsley, oregano, basil, and bay leaves. If making the Bar-B-Q Spaghetti, add the pork shoulder and Bar-B-Q sauce at this stage.

Simmer the sauce over low heat for 15 minutes. Remove the bay leaves and discard. Continue simmering the sauce to allow the flavors to meld, about 45 minutes longer. Taste the sauce and adjust the seasoning, adding sugar if the tomatoes are too acidic or garlic powder if the garlic flavor isn't strong enough. Allow the sauce continue simmering—the longer the better. Serve over spaghetti noodles, cooked according to package directions.

GRITS N' Q

If you like shrimp and grits, you'll love Grits n' Q. The creamy grits marry perfectly with the saucy pork. Serve this dish as a main course at brunch, or as a hearty entrée for an evening meal.

YIELDS: 6 servings

CORKY'S FAMILY: Rebecca Jones

1 cup grits *(instant, quick-cooking, or stone-ground)*

½ cup (1 stick) unsalted butter

½ teaspoon salt

2 large eggs, beaten

1 cup milk

4 ounces processed cheese, cubed

1 cup (4 ounces) shredded Cheddar cheese

3 dashes hot sauce *(Tabasco preferred)*

1 pound Corky's Bar-B-Q Pork Shoulder

½ cup Corky's Original Recipe Bar-B-Q Sauce

Preheat the oven to 350°F. In a large saucepan, cook the grits according to package directions. Take the pan off the heat, add the butter and salt and stir to melt the butter.

In a medium bowl, whisk the eggs and add the milk. Whisk a large dollop of the hot grits into the egg mixture to temper. Slowly add the milk and egg mixture to grits while stirring. Add the processed cheese, Cheddar cheese, and hot sauce to the grits and stir until the cheese melts. Place the Bar-B-Q Pork Shoulder in the bottom of a cast-iron skillet or oven-safe baking dish. Pour the Bar-B-Q sauce over the pork and top with the cheese grits. Bake uncovered until heated through and browned on top, about 40 to 45 minutes.

TACOS THE MEMPHIS WAY

Consider a taco bar for your next gathering. Guests will love eating what they want, how they want it. It's easy for the host, too. Add more condiments if you like, such as chopped fresh cilantro, sour cream, mashed avocado, or sliced black olives.

YIELDS: 4 to 6 servings

CORKY'S FAMILY: Sheila Thomas

2 cups (8 ounces) shredded Cheddar cheese

1 cup shredded iceberg lettuce

2 medium tomatoes, chopped

½ cup chopped green onions (from about 6 green onions)

2 medium jalapeño peppers, seeded and chopped

1 pound Corky's Bar-B-Q Pulled Pork or Chicken

1 (15-ounce) can black beans, drained and rinsed

12 soft-taco-size flour tortillas

1 (18-ounce) bottle Corky's Original Recipe Bar-B-Q Sauce

Preheat the oven to 350°F. Place the cheese and vegetables in separate serving bowls for quick assembly of tacos. Place the meat in a covered, oven-safe container and wrap the tortillas foil. Warm both the meat and the tortillas in the oven. (For even tastier tortillas, warm individually on a griddle pan on the stovetop.) Heat the black beans either in a small pot set over medium-low heat or in the microwave. Serve buffet style or plate individually. To serve, spoon some meat and beans down the center of each tortilla, and top with the cheese, vegetables, and Bar-B-Q sauce.

BROTHER AL'S SOUTHERN FRIED CHICKEN

Although we don't serve fried chicken on our menu, when the staff needs a change from pulled pork, Brother Al will whip up his famous spicy fried chicken for the back-of-house meal. He has graciously allowed us to reprint his secrets here.

YIELDS: 8 servings

CORKY'S FAMILY: Al Palmer

1 (1-pound) can vegetable shortening *(for frying)*

4 large eggs

⅓ cup water

½ cup (4 ounces) hot red pepper sauce *(preferably Louisiana Hot Sauce)*

2 cups self-rising flour

2 tablespoons Corky's Bar-B-Q Dry Rub

1 tablespoon freshly ground black pepper

2½ pounds bone-in chicken pieces

1 teaspoon salt

In a large cast iron skillet or pot, heat the shortening until it reaches 350°F. Combine the eggs with ⅓ cup of water and the hot sauce in a shallow dish and beat with a fork to blend. In a separate shallow dish, mix together the flour, dry rub, and pepper.

Dip the chicken in the egg mixture and then coat in the flour mixture. Carefully lay the chicken in the hot shortening, taking care not to crowd the pan. Fry the chicken until it is cooked through, flipping once, about 10 to 12 minutes. Drain on a wire rack, sprinkling with salt while still warm. Serve hot or cold.

> Our customers love Corky's barbecue because it's good ol' comfort food. They're bringing the South to your home. It's authentic, and it tastes just _that_ good.
>
> — *Lauren Baker, QVC*

BRANDON'S CHICKEN POT PIE

If you don't have grilled chicken breasts handy, you can use canned chicken or the meat from a rotisserie chicken (you'll need about 4 cups total). For a smoky flavor, sprinkle Corky's Bar-B-Q Dry Rub on the crust before baking.

YIELDS: 6 servings

CORKY'S FRIEND: Brandon Pelts

½ **large onion, diced** *(about 1½ cups)*

2 **large carrots, peeled and sliced** *(about 1 cup)*

2 **large celery ribs, sliced** *(about 1 cup)*

½ **cup green peas**

⅓ **cup (5⅓ tablespoons) unsalted butter**

⅓ **cup all-purpose flour**

1¾ **cups chicken broth**

½ **cup heavy whipping cream**

½ **teaspoon freshly ground black pepper**

½ **teaspoon dried thyme**

½ **teaspoon dried sage**

Nonstick cooking spray, oil, or butter

1 **(2-count) package refrigerated pie crusts**

4 **boneless chicken breasts, cooked and chopped**

Corky's Bar-B-Q Dry Rub *(optional)*

Preheat the oven to 425°F. Bring a medium pot of salted water to a boil over high heat. Add the onion, carrots, celery, and peas and cook, covered, until crisp-tender, about 5 minutes. Drain well.

In another medium saucepan over medium heat, melt the butter. Add the flour and cook, stirring, until the mixture is golden brown. Slowly add the chicken broth and cream and bring to a boil, stirring constantly. Reduce the heat to a simmer and season with the pepper, thyme, and sage. Cook, stirring, until mixture is thickened and smooth, about 5 minutes longer. Stir in the cooked vegetables and set aside.

Using the nonstick spray, oil, or butter, grease a 9-inch pie pan. Place the bottom pie crust into the prepared pan. Add the chicken and cover with the sauce. Top with the second pie crust and crimp the edges to seal. Cut small holes in the top to vent. Bake the pot pie until golden brown and bubbling, about 30 to 40 minutes. (If the edges are browning too quickly, cover them with aluminum foil.)

MISSISSIPPI DELTA HOPPIN' JOHN

This quick and easy version of a Southern tradition is often requested by the Cordova employees. It's been a back-of-house favorite since the first time Peggy made it for a staff dinner. Some of us even add hushpuppies to it when serving.

YIELDS: 8 servings

CORKY'S FAMILY: Peggy Williams

2 (15-ounce) cans black-eyed peas, drained and rinsed

2 cups diced cooked or smoked ham

1 (10-ounce) can diced tomatoes and green chilies (*Ro*Tel preferred*)

4 cups cooked white rice

Combine the black-eyed peas, ham, and tomatoes and chilies in a heavy-bottomed saucepan over medium heat. Cook, covered, until heated through and flavors meld, about 45 minutes. Serve over the white rice.

Every year I send my customers a batch of Corky's ribs for the holidays. I've started a trend that I can't stop: They love them and always look for them come December. One year, our largest customer made some internal changes and dropped us as a vendor in the process. They were an important customer, and this change greatly reduced our income. As a joke, I asked Corky's to forgo the ribs for that customer and send them a box of bones. That's right—delicious Corky's ribs, but this time sans meat. Corky's played along and overnighted them. The customer called me right away and asked what the heck was going on. I told him that business was so bad, I couldn't afford to send them ribs. Of course, the next day, another rack arrived, this time with the meat. Since then, that director left the company and has gone elsewhere. We got the job back at his original company and the director awarded us the business at his new company, too. They're now our two largest clients.

— *Wes Kraker, life-long Corky's customer, Memphis, TN*

CHICKEN TOMATO PIE

Don't skip this recipe just because you don't have a Corky's Bar-B-Q Chicken! Though we love the smoky taste of the Corky's chicken, this pie works equally well with leftover chicken or the meat from a rotisserie. To make the tomatoes easier to peel, cut an "X" into the bottom of each one and dip them in boiling water for 1 minute.

YIELDS: 8 servings

CORKY'S FAMILY: Carol Sweeney

4 medium tomatoes

1 unbaked deep-dish pie crust

¼ cup herb-flavored cream cheese, softened

½ pound Corky's Bar-B-Q Pulled Chicken, chopped *(about 1 cup)*

1 small red onion, diced *(about 1 cup)*

2 tablespoons fresh dill or ¾ teaspoon dried dill

Salt and freshly ground black pepper *(to taste)*

2 cups (8 ounces) shredded Cheddar cheese

1 cup mayonnaise

Preheat the oven to 350°F. Peel and slice the tomatoes, sprinkle with salt, and let sit on paper towels for 30 minutes to drain. Line a pie crust (in its foil pan or in your own pie dish) with parchment paper and pie weights or dry beans, and bake just until the sides are set, about 15 minutes. Remove the crust from the oven, and remove the pie weights and parchment from the crust. Evenly spread the herb cream cheese over the bottom of the baked pie crust. Add the chicken and follow with a layer of tomatoes. Sprinkle with the diced red onion and dill and follow with another layer of tomatoes. Repeat the red onion, dill, and tomato layers until the crust is full. Combine the Cheddar cheese and mayonnaise and spread over the top of the pie (hands will work well for this task). Bake until the cheese is melted and the pie is beginning to brown, about 25 minutes. Let cool 5 minutes before serving.

NITA'S ROASTED CHICKEN

Instead of roasting, you can cook this in the crockpot on low for 8 hours.

YIELDS: 5 servings

CORKY'S FAMILY: Anita Brown Patrick

5 teaspoons Corky's Bar-B-Q Dry Rub

1 teaspoon cayenne pepper

1 teaspoon onion powder

1 teaspoon dried thyme

1 teaspoon white pepper

½ teaspoon freshly ground black pepper

1 (3- to 5-pound) roasting chicken

1 small onion, quartered

In a small bowl, combine the dry rub with all the spices. Remove the giblets from the chicken, clean the cavity well, and pat dry with paper towels. Rub the spice mixture onto the chicken, both inside and out, making sure it is evenly distributed and massaged into the skin. Place the chicken in a resealable plastic bag, seal, and refrigerate overnight.

Before roasting the chicken, preheat the oven to 250°F. Stuff the onion in the bird's cavity and place the chicken in a shallow baking pan. Roast uncovered until golden brown, fragrant, and tender, about 5 hours. After the first hour, baste the chicken occasionally with its pan juices. Let rest 15 minutes before carving.

ZESTY PULLED BAR-B-Q CHICKEN

Served on its own, or as a sandwich, this flavorful, tender chicken is easy and delicious.

YIELDS: 6 servings

CORKY'S FRIEND: Laurie Karchmer

6 boneless, skinless chicken breast halves

1 (18-ounce) bottle Corky's Original Recipe Bar-B-Q Sauce

½ cup bottled Italian-style vinaigrette

¼ cup lightly packed brown sugar

2 tablespoons Worcestershire sauce

Place the chicken in a crock-pot. Whisk the Corky's Bar-B-Q sauce, Italian vinaigrette, brown sugar, and Worcestershire sauce together in a bowl and pour over the chicken. Cover and cook on low until very tender, about 6 to 8 hours. When done cooking, take 2 forks and shred the meat into small pieces.

CORKY'S CHICKEN ENCHILADAS

Try Corky's pulled pork or rotisserie chicken as a variation.

YIELDS: 6 servings

CORKY'S FAMILY: Mary Shamblin

1 pound Corky's Bar-B-Q Pulled Chicken (about 2 cups)

1 (16-ounce) can refried beans

1 (10.75-ounce) can condensed Cheddar cheese soup

1 medium onion, chopped (about 1½ cups)

1 cup cooked rice

1 tablespoon Corky's Bar-B-Q Dry Rub

6 large flour tortillas

1½ cups enchilada sauce (about 12 ounces)

2 cups (8 ounces) shredded Cheddar cheese

Chopped tomatoes, cilantro, and green onion (for garnish)

Preheat the oven to 350°F. In a large skillet over medium heat, combine the chicken, beans, soup, onion, rice, and dry rub. Cook, stirring occasionally, until heated through. Divide the mixture evenly between the tortillas. Roll up the tortillas and place them, seam-side down, in a shallow baking dish. Pour the enchilada sauce over the tortillas and sprinkle with the cheese. Bake until the enchiladas are bubbling, about 20 minutes. Garnish with tomatoes, cilantro, and green onion.

AZELY'S GRILLED BAR-B-Q CHICKEN

AC, or Azely, the singing server, has been entertaining guests since the doors opened in 1984.

YIELDS: 4 servings
CORKY'S FRIEND: Azely Jackson

2 tablespoons olive oil

1 tablespoon garlic powder

1 teaspoon Corky's Bar-B-Q Dry Rub

8 pieces bone-in chicken, skin removed

Corky's Original Recipe Bar-B-Q Sauce *(for serving)*

Prepare a grill for medium-heat cooking. In a small bowl, combine the olive oil, garlic powder, and dry rub. Lightly brush the chicken pieces with mixture. Grill the chicken over medium heat until done, about 12 to 15 minutes. Brush the chicken with Corky's Original Bar-B-Q Sauce before serving.

BILLIE'S DRY-RUBBED RIB-EYES

The secret to Corky's Bar-B-Q is low, slow cooking. These rib-eyes have all the flavor of Corky's famous rub, but will cook up in no time. For best results, rub them with the seasoning the day before to give the spices time to penetrate the meat.

YIELDS: 4 servings
CORKY'S FAMILY: Billie Pelts

3 tablespoons Corky's Bar-B-Q Dry Rub

1 teaspoon ground cumin

4 rib-eye steaks, about 1½ inches thick

2 tablespoons canola oil

1 teaspoon salt

Prepare a grill for high-heat cooking. In a small bowl, combine the dry rub and cumin, stirring to mix well. Drizzle the rib-eyes with the canola oil and rub to coat evenly. Season the steaks with the salt, and then sprinkle with the spice mixture on both sides. Grill the steaks on high to sear, turning once, about 5 minutes. Lower the heat (or move to a cooler part of the grill) and cook the steaks to the desired degree of doneness, turning once, about 8 to 12 minutes.

ROSE'S BRISKET

"I like to use smoke when I'm finishing the brisket. It flavors the sauce and makes everyone think you're a real-deal Bar-B-Q chef, with all that aroma and smoke coming from the grill," says recipe contributor Rocky Waite. "Serve the brisket sliced on a plate as a main course, or chop and serve on buns or rolls for a backyard party. To reheat leftovers, wrap in foil with some extra sauce for moisture, and heat in a 300°F oven until warmed throughout."

YIELDS: 15 servings
CORKY'S FRIEND: Rocky Waite

8 pounds beef brisket

Garlic powder

1 (2.5-ounce) bottle Corky's Bar-B-Q Dry Rub, divided

1½ cups red or white wine

1 (18-ounce) bottle Corky's Original Recipe Bar-B-Q Sauce, divided

Trim the excess fat from the brisket, saving the trimmings. Liberally season the brisket with garlic powder and dry rub, and massage it into the meat. Place the brisket in a roasting pan, cover with plastic wrap, and refrigerate for 3 to 4 hours.

About 3½ hours before you plan to serve the brisket, prepare a grill for low-heat cooking (approximately 275°F.) Place the brisket atop a sheet of heavy-duty aluminum foil (the foil should be large enough to enclose the entire brisket). Place reserved fat trimmings on top of the brisket and seal the aluminum foil on top and on one end, folding and crimping edges securely. Carefully pour the wine into the open end of the packet, and then seal tightly.

Continued

Rose's Brisket continued

Place the wrapped brisket on the grill, away from the coals if possible, and cook for 2½ to 3 hours. Carefully remove the foil, pouring the juices into a large glass measuring cup to reserve. Discard the fat pieces (or create smoke by placing them onto the grill to drip onto the coals). Place the brisket onto the grill, seasoned-side down, directly over the coals. Add wood chips to the coals to raise the heat to 325°F to create lots of smoke. When the seasoned side has a browned, crispy crust, turn the brisket over and add a coating of dry rub. Brush on a heavy coating of Bar-B-Q sauce and cook until the sauce becomes dark and thick.

Remove the brisket from the grill, place on a cutting board, and tent with foil. Let the brisket sit for at least 15 minutes. Slice against the grain into ¼-inch-thick pieces with a serrated or electric knife. Place the brisket on a serving platter.

Bring the reserved cooking juices to a boil in a small saucepan and reduce slightly. Serve the juices with the meat.

MEEMAW'S BRISKET

YIELDS: 6 to 8 servings
CORKY'S FAMILY: Linda Pelts

1 (12-ounce) bottle chili sauce

¾ cup white wine vinegar

1 teaspoon chopped garlic

¾ cup lightly packed brown sugar

5 pounds beef brisket, with fat cap

Salt and freshly ground black pepper *(to taste)*

3 large onions, sliced

In a medium bowl, mix together the chili sauce, vinegar, garlic, and brown sugar. Place the brisket in a roasting pan, fat-side up, and season liberally with salt and pepper. Scatter the onion slices over the brisket, and then top with the vinegar mixture. Cover and refrigerate overnight.

Preheat the oven to 325°F. Cook uncovered for 1 hour, basting often with marinade. Cover tightly with foil and continue to cook until fork-tender, about 3 hours. Let rest before slicing against the grain. Serve the brisket with pan juices.

DILL TARTAR SAUCE

 YIELDS: 16 servings

1 cup mayonnaise

½ cup dill relish

½ cup chopped onion *(from about ½ small onion)*

1 tablespoon salt

1 teaspoon garlic powder

1 teaspoon freshly ground black pepper

Mix all ingredients together in a small bowl. Cover and refrigerate until ready to serve.

KT'S SOUTHERN FRIED CATFISH

KT is a man of many names as well as many culinary talents. Whether you call him KT, Kevin Turner, or Gucci, you can always find him at one of the Corky's locations cooking up some Southern perfection like this fried catfish. Feel free to substitute tilapia or other mild white fish for equally delicious results.

YIELDS: 4 servings

CORKY'S FAMILY: Kevin Turner

Canola oil (for frying)

1⅓ cups cornmeal

⅔ cup all-purpose flour

1 tablespoon salt

1 teaspoon ground red pepper

1 cup milk

1 large egg, lightly beaten

4 catfish fillets

Dill Tartar Sauce *(page 192)*

In a large pot, Dutch oven, or electric fryer, heat at least 2 inches of oil to 375°F over medium-high heat. Mix the cornmeal, flour, salt, and pepper together in a large shallow dish and whisk the milk and egg together in a separate shallow bowl. Dip the catfish first in the egg and milk mixture, allowing the excess to drip off, and then dredge in the cornmeal mixture, shaking to remove any excess.

To see if the oil is hot enough, sprinkle a tiny pinch of cornmeal into the oil. If it bubbles, it's ready. Carefully add 2 catfish fillets to the oil. Adjust the heat as needed to maintain the oil at 375°F. Fry the catfish, turning once, until golden brown and the fish flakes easily when tested with a fork, about 3 to 4 minutes per side. Using slotted spoon, transfer the catfish to paper-towel-lined plate to drain. Remove any large bits of crust from the oil. Fry the remaining fish. Serve immediately with the tartar sauce.

BAR-B-Q SHRIMP TWO WAYS

The Southern Way

YIELDS: 6 servings
CORKY'S FRIEND: Tommy Gerber

1 cup (2 sticks) unsalted butter

½ cup freshly squeezed lime juice
(from about 4 to 6 limes)

4 sprigs fresh thyme

2 tablespoons Worcestershire sauce

1 tablespoon hot sauce

2 teaspoons freshly ground black pepper

2 teaspoons kosher salt

2 pounds extra-jumbo shrimp
(16 to 20 per pound), shell on

3 tablespoons olive oil, divided

3 tablespoons chopped flat leaf parsley

1 loaf French bread

Salt and freshly ground black pepper
(to taste)

If using a grill, prepare for medium-heat cooking. In a heavy-bottomed pot (set right on the grill or on the stovetop over medium heat), combine the butter, lime juice, thyme, Worcestershire sauce, hot sauce, pepper, and salt. Cook until the butter has melted and the mixture begins to simmer. Add the shrimp and toss to coat with the sauce. Let cook 2 to 3 minutes until pink and done. Remove from the heat and stir in the parsley.

Tommy's Way

Cut the bread in half lengthwise, drizzle with the remaining tablespoon of olive oil, sprinkle with the salt and pepper, and place cut-side down on the grill until toasted, about 1 to 2 minutes. Serve alongside the shrimp.

The Southern Way

Serve the shrimp over barbecued Peabody Potatoes (page 160), a decadent, creamy dish of fluffy potatoes swirled with spicy barbecue sauce.

CORKY'S SLANG

Don Pelts, known fondly as "Capt'n or Capt'n D" by the Corky's crew, has a language all his own. Corky's employees know exactly what he means. Do you?

BACKSIDE!:

Get out of my way, I'm coming behind you! *(Probably with a big tray of barbecue, beans, and slaw.)*

SLAP DOWN:

When you do a great job, you are looking for a "slap down" from Don Pelts: an on-the-spot cash bonus or a gorgeous looking rib straight off the grill.

NEED IT ON THE HEE-HAW:

A customer is waiting too long or we need the food ASAP. When employees hear that someone needs it "on the hee-haw," everyone jumps immediately to get this order expedited before anything else.

TAKE IT TO THE CRIB:

Don started using this phrase when he was on the late-night closing shift for the restaurant. It means let's get out of here and head back to the house and go to bed.

BARNYARD PIMP:

How the kitchen identifies a chicken order. As in, "Give me a barnyard pimp on the hee-haw."

GRILLED PINEAPPLE BAR-B-Q SALMON

YIELDS: 4 servings

CORKY'S FAMILY: Billie Pelts

1 15-inch cedar plank

1 (1½-pound) salmon fillet

½ cup pineapple juice

2 tablespoons Corky's Bar-B-Q Dry Rub

1 tablespoon ground cumin

Salt and freshly ground black pepper *(to taste)*

Soak the cedar plank in water for at least 30 minutes. Place the salmon fillet in a large glass baking dish and pour the pineapple juice over it; allow the salmon to marinate for 30 minutes.

Meanwhile, preheat the grill to medium-low heat. Remove the salmon from the marinade and coat the salmon with the dry rub and ground cumin, then sprinkle it with salt and pepper. Place the soaked plank on the grill, and close the lid for 3 minutes to heat the plank. Carefully turn the plank over, and place the salmon skin-side down directly on the heated side of the plank and close the lid. Grill until the desired degree of doneness is reached, about 12 to 15 minutes.

GRILLED LEMONS

Grilled lemons add a robust citrus flavor to sauces, dressings, vegetables, meats, and fish.

Lemon slices or halves

Grill the lemon slices or halves until charred, turning the slices once. To enhance the natural caramelization process, sprinkle sugar on the lemon slices prior to grilling.

BAKED BAR-B-Q SALMON

This dish is quick to make and very tasty, yet low in fat and packed with essential Omega-3s. Try this can't-miss recipe for a family dinner.

YIELDS: 4 servings

CORKY'S FRIEND: Sherrie Senft

1 (2-pound) salmon fillet

¼ cup freshly squeezed lemon juice *(from about 1 to 2 lemons)*

2 tablespoons thinly sliced fresh basil

1 tablespoon minced fresh parsley

1 teaspoon minced fresh oregano

1 teaspoon freshly ground black pepper

1 cup Corky's Original Recipe Bar-B-Q Sauce

Preheat the oven to 450°F. Place the salmon fillet in a 13 x 9-inch pan, skin-side down. Pour the lemon juice over the salmon fillet, then sprinkle with the fresh herbs and pepper. Bake for 5 minutes. Remove the salmon from the oven and slather it with the Bar-B-Q sauce. Return the salmon to the oven and continue baking until the salmon is cooked through and flakes easily with a fork, about 10 to 12 minutes longer.

> Corky's is a regular stop any time I get to Arkansas or Tennessee—which isn't nearly often enough! They have awesome food, superior service, tender meat, and down-home service. I even sent my nephew a rack of ribs for his 16th birthday. He loved them!
>
> — *Sherrie Senft,*
> *long-time fan of Corky's*

SHRIMP AND GRITS

Plump shrimp, rich gravy, and creamy grits capture the spirit of low-country cooking.

YIELDS: 4 to 6 servings

CORKY'S FRIEND: Andy Feinstone

1 teaspoon olive oil

4 slices smoked thick-cut bacon, diced

¼ cup diced green bell pepper *(from about ¼ green bell pepper)*

¼ cup diced red bell pepper *(from about ¼ red bell pepper)*

2 tablespoons chopped garlic

1 green onion, thinly sliced

1 pound shrimp, peeled and deveined

3 tablespoons all-purpose flour

1 cup heavy whipping cream

¼ teaspoon cayenne pepper

1 cup whole milk

1 cup water

¼ cup (½ stick) unsalted butter

¾ cup quick-cooking grits

¾ cup (3 ounces) grated sharp Cheddar cheese

Salt and freshly ground black pepper *(to taste)*

To prepare the shrimp, pour the oil into a large, heavy-bottomed sauté pan over medium heat. Add the bacon, peppers, garlic, and green onion and sauté until the bacon is crisp. Add the shrimp and sauté just until cooked through. Dust the shrimp mixture with flour and stir well. Add the heavy cream and cayenne and bring to a simmer, then reduce heat to low and simmer gently until sauce thickens, about 2 minutes.

Combine the milk, 1 cup water, and butter in a small saucepan over medium heat. Bring to a simmer and add the grits. Cover and cook until the grits are tender, about 5 minutes, and then stir in the cheese to melt. Season to taste with salt and pepper. Spoon the shrimp over the grits and serve.

I love the dry ribs. My favorite way is "muddy." You take a rack of wet ribs and let them warm real slow until the sauce caramelizes, or you can put them under the broiler for a more charred effect. Then you sprinkle the sticky sauce with the dry rub. Muddy. Yummy.

— *Robbie Levine, Corky's*
employee since day one

CAKES, SHAKES, CRUMBLES, & PIES

IN MEMPHIS WE'RE PARTIAL TO PECAN PIE, BUTTERMILK PIE, AND COBBLERS OF ALL KINDS. OH YES WE ALSO ENJOY A RICH CHOCOLATE FUDGE PIE. AND CAN'T FORGET STRAWBERRY CAKE OR 'BANANA' PUDDING - THAT'S A MUST. SUFFICE IT TO SAY, OUR SWEET TOOTH KNOWS FEW LIMITS, AS YOU'LL FIND IN A QUICK PERUSAL OF THIS CHAPTER.

Nancy's Blackberry Cobbler

Southern Pecan Pie

Homemade Vanilla Ice Cream

MOMO'S HOT FUDGE SAUCE

We believe that all savory things taste better with bacon and that everything sweet is better with Momo's Fudge Sauce. Therefore, we begin this sweet section with this key recipe, passed down to Linda Pelts from her mother-in-law. "Don's mom, Momo, was the ultimate matriarch of the family, the Queen of the Pelts Clan," says Linda. "She held court every Friday with a family dinner at her house. She and her dinners were well-loved, but what the family loved most was getting to eat her weekly batch of homemade hot fudge, poured over Klinke Brothers vanilla ice cream, made just down the road off I-240."

YIELDS: 12 servings

CORKY'S FAMILY: Linda Pelts

½ **cup (1 stick) unsalted butter** *(no substitutions)*

4 (1-ounce) squares unsweetened chocolate *(Baker's preferred)*

2 cups granulated sugar

1 (12-ounce) can evaporated milk

Pinch of salt

1½ teaspoons vanilla extract

In a heavy-bottomed pot set over medium-low heat, gently melt the butter and chocolate together, stirring with a wooden spoon. Slowly add the sugar, evaporated milk, and salt and continue stirring until the mixture thickens and begins to boil, about 10 to 15 minutes. Allow to cool before adding the vanilla.

Store, covered, in the refrigerator for up to 2 weeks or in the freezer for up to 3 months. Reheat in the microwave or a warm water bath.

BREAKING NEWS: This is the first time this recipe is being given out past the family.

Almost Miss Linda's Fudge Pie with
Momo's Hot Fudge Sauce

ALMOST MISS LINDA'S FUDGE PIE

Carol Sweeney has worked for Corky's since she was 16. This recipe is her rendition of Corky's famously decadent fudge pie, first created by Linda Pelts, the wife of Corky's founder Don Pelts. Of special note: this the pie makes it own crust!

YIELDS: 8 servings

CORKY'S FAMILY: Carol Sweeney

Nonstick cooking spray, oil, or butter

1 cup all-purpose flour, plus additional flour for the pan

2 cups sugar

½ cup unsweetened cocoa powder

1 cup (2 sticks) unsalted butter, melted

3 large eggs

½ teaspoon vanilla extract

½ cup chopped pecans

Preheat the oven to 375°F. Using nonstick spray, oil, or butter, grease and flour an 8-inch pie pan. Sift together the sugar, 1 cup flour, and the cocoa in a large mixing bowl. Add the melted butter and mix well. Using a mixer set on low speed, mix in the eggs and vanilla until just blended, taking care not to overbeat. Stir in the pecans. Pour the mixture into the prepared pie pan and bake until just set in center, about 45 to 50 minutes.

I remember when my mom made every single pie served at Corky's. It seemed like every time I walked into our kitchen at home, I was met with rows and rows of fudge pies and pecan pies. Seriously—I remember seeing 40 covering every bare surface in the kitchen and dining room. We placed an order for 24,000 pies last week, so I'm sure she was thrilled when we finally outsourced the pies to a professional baker.

— Tricia Woodman, daughter of Corky's founder

BEN'S MOM'S ALMOND PEACH PIE

YIELDS: 8 servings

CORKY'S FAMILY: Ben Horton

10 tablespoons (1¼ sticks) unsalted butter or margarine, divided

⅓ cup finely crushed vanilla wafers *(from about 7 to 8 wafers)*

¼ cup chopped almonds

1 cup sugar

2 tablespoons all-purpose flour

2 eggs, beaten

¼ teaspoon almond extract

6 to 8 medium peaches, peeled, pitted, and sliced

1 (9-inch) unbaked pie crust

Vanilla ice cream or whipped cream *(for serving)*

Preheat the oven to 400°F. In medium-size microwave-safe bowl, microwave 2 tablespoons of the butter or margarine until melted. Add the wafers and almonds to the melted butter and stir to combine; set aside. In a small saucepan set over low heat, melt the remaining 8 tablespoons of butter. Add the sugar and flour; beat in the eggs and cook on low heat for 3 to 5 minutes, stirring often. Remove from the heat and stir in the almond extract.

Arrange the peaches in the pie crust and pour the butter mixture over them. Sprinkle the wafer mixture over the top. Bake for 8 minutes, then reduce the heat to 350°F and bake until the filling bubbles and the top is golden brown, about 45 minutes longer. Serve warm with vanilla ice cream or whipped cream. Store, covered, in the refrigerator.

I know Jimmy from Corky's because we're both on-air guests at QVC. He showcases barbecue and I cover desserts with cookies and brownies from Cheryl's. Since I live in Ohio, the QVC campus in Pennsylvania is the first place I ever tried Corky's. The meat is so tender—it falls off the bone and is everything he says it is on the air. I can't wait to try it from the restaurant in Memphis some day.

— *Mary Eckenrode, QVC personality and Corky's fan*

PEANUT BUTTER AND FUDGE PIE

Some things are just meant to be together, like beans and slaw. Peanut butter and fudge is an obvious combination, and one with uncommonly good results.

YIELDS: 8 servings

CORKY'S FAMILY: Carol Sweeney

Nonstick cooking spray, oil, or butter

1 cup all-purpose flour, plus additional flour for the pan

2 cups sugar

½ cup unsweetened cocoa powder

1 cup (2 sticks) unsalted butter, melted

3 large eggs

½ teaspoon vanilla extract

½ cup chopped pecans

¼ cup creamy peanut butter

Preheat the oven to 375°F. Using nonstick cooking spray, oil, or butter, grease and flour an 8-inch pie pan.

Sift together the sugar, 1 cup flour, and cocoa in a large mixing bowl. Add the melted butter, and mix well. Using a mixer set on low speed, mix in the eggs and vanilla until just blended, taking care not to overbeat. Stir in the pecans. Pour half of the chocolate batter into the prepared pie pan. Spoon the peanut butter over the batter and follow with the remaining chocolate batter. Swirl the batter gently with a knife to create patterns. Bake until just set in center, about 45 to 50 minutes.

Jimmy with David Venable, host of QVC's popular show, In the Kitchen with David.

S'MORES PIE

This recipe is a can't-miss family favorite. We had to make it on two separate occasions just to get this photograph—the first one out of the oven was so irresistible that it disappeared before we could get the shot.

YIELDS: 8 servings

CORKY'S FAMILY: Ann Keyes

1½ cups milk chocolate chips

1½ cups dark chocolate chips

1½ cups heavy whipping cream, divided

1 (9-ounce) graham cracker pie crust

2 cups large marshmallows

2 cups miniature marshmallows

½ cup sweetened condensed milk

Place the chocolate chips in a large microwaveable bowl with ½ cup of the heavy whipping cream. Microwave on high, uncovered, in 30-second intervals, stirring between, until the chocolate chips are completely melted and the mixture is smooth.

Place the remaining 1 cup of heavy whipping cream in a mixing bowl with the melted chocolate. Beat with an electric mixer set on high speed until thick. Spread the mixture in the graham cracker crust and refrigerate for at least 2 hours.

Just before serving, arrange the oven rack 5 inches below the broiler, and preheat the broiler. Arrange all of the marshmallows on top of the pie and drizzle with the sweetened condensed milk. Broil the pie, leaving the oven door open slightly and watching carefully so the pie does not burn, until the marshmallows turn golden brown. Serve immediately. (To slice the pie more easily, run a serrated knife under hot water before cutting.)

BIG MAMA'S LEMON MERINGUE PIE

"Like so many Southern grandmothers, mine was a great cook. So well loved was her Lemon Meringue Pie that my mother and several cousins requested one in lieu of a birthday cake at the family celebration," says Sheila Thomas. "Big Mama's Lemon Meringue Pie was not just the best-tasting pie in town, it was also the most beautiful, with perfect swirly meringue that seemed to be a mile high—no small feat in Memphis humidity, to be sure."

YIELDS: 8 servings

CORKY'S FAMILY: Sheila Thomas

Pie

2 large lemons

3 large eggs, separated, whites reserved for meringue

1 cup sugar

3 tablespoons all-purpose flour

3 tablespoons cornstarch

⅛ teaspoon salt

1½ cups hot water

2 tablespoons (¼ stick) unsalted butter

1 (9-inch) pie crust, baked

Meringue

1 tablespoon cornstarch

⅓ cup hot water

3 egg whites (reserved from pie recipe), at room temperature

¼ teaspoon cream of tartar

6 tablespoons sugar

For filling: Wash and dry the lemons. Zest one lemon, then juice both, measuring out ⅓ cup of juice. In a small bowl, lightly beat the egg yolks. In a medium saucepan, mix together the sugar, flour, cornstarch, and salt. Set over low heat and add the 1½ cups of hot water slowly, stirring constantly, until the mixture begins to thicken. Stir in a small amount of the hot mixture to the beaten egg yolks to temper them and then add the yolk mixture to the pan. Gently stir and cook until thickened, about 2 minutes longer. Remove from the heat and mix in the butter, ⅓ cup lemon juice, and lemon zest. Pour the filling into the baked pie shell and refrigerate until thoroughly cooled, at least 2 hours.

For meringue: Preheat the oven to 325°F. Begin by stirring the cornstarch into the water to create a thick gel. In a large metal or glass mixing bowl, beat the reserved egg whites together with the cream of tartar. Add the cornstarch gel one teaspoonful at a time, continuing to beat. When soft peaks begin to form, add the sugar, one tablespoon at a time, beating until the peaks do not fall when the beater is lifted.

Spoon the meringue onto the cooled pie, using a spatula to create beautiful peaks. Place the pie in the oven and bake until golden brown, taking care not to overcook the meringue, about 20 to 25 minutes.

SOUTHERN PECAN PIE

Pecan pie ranks right up there with magnolias and sweet tea as a quintessential Southern favorite. This recipe comes courtesy of Memphis' own Andy Feinstone, owner of Boscos restaurants around town.

YIELDS: 8 servings

CORKY'S FRIEND: Andy Feinstone

1 cup dark corn syrup *(or a combination of dark and light)*

4 eggs, beaten

¾ cup sugar

¼ cup (½ stick) unsalted butter, melted

1½ teaspoons vanilla extract

1½ cups coarsely chopped pecans

1 (9-inch) unbaked deep-dish pie crust

½ teaspoon salt

Vanilla ice cream *(for serving)*

Caramel or chocolate sauce *(for serving)*

Preheat the oven to 350°F. In a large bowl, mix together the corn syrup, eggs, sugar, melted butter, and vanilla. Stir in the chopped pecans and pour into unbaked pie crust.

Bake the pie on the middle rack of the oven until the center is set, about 1 hour. Allow to cool completely and serve with vanilla ice cream and caramel or chocolate sauce.

My family and I went on a rib tour a few years ago and ate at 15 different places across five states. Corky's was by far the best of the bunch. If you're touring Memphis, I highly recommend a stop there.

— *a review from Willie, Westminster, CO*

BUTTERMILK PIE

Every Southern cookbook must have a buttermilk pie. This sugary custard is so simple, yet it tastes so good.

YIELDS: 8 servings

CORKY'S FRIEND: Charles Free

1½ cups sugar

¼ cup (½ stick) unsalted butter, softened

3 large eggs, beaten

1 cup buttermilk

1 tablespoon all-purpose flour

1 teaspoon vanilla extract

1 (9-inch) unbaked pie crust

Preheat the oven to 350°F. In large bowl, cream the sugar and butter together until smooth. Add the eggs, beating to combine, then add the buttermilk, flour, and vanilla, and beat to combine well. Pour the filling into the pie crust and bake until the center of the pie is set, about 30 minutes.

Christmas is and always will be my favorite holiday. What's a holiday without family traditions? Keeping those traditions going is not an easy task when you have to move your family half-way across the country, though. That is what happened to the Cobb clan in the early 1980s. We moved from our home of 20 years in Southaven, Mississippi, a suburb of Memphis, to Dallas, Texas, some 900 miles away. Settling in a new city is never easy, especially during the holidays when you're far away from friends and extended family. I think it was around 1987 when my dad thought of a way to bring a part of Memphis to us for Christmas. He surprised us all by having Corky's BBQ shipped in for our Christmas Eve dinner. You have to remember that, back then, you couldn't get pork BBQ anywhere in north Texas, the land of beef. Thanks to FedEx, good Corky's BBQ was no longer a treat we only got to enjoy when we went home. A new tradition was born. While my dad is no longer with us, we have kept up the tradition and feel he's still a part of our Christmas Eve celebration. Thanks, Corky's, for the Cobb's Corky Christmas Eve tradition!

— *Renee Cobb Morris, life-long customer, Dallas, TX*

ZACHARY'S APPLE DUMPLINGS

A dessert made with Mountain Dew? Yes, indeed! It's super-easy and always a crowd pleaser. Try it on your brunch buffet, as well as for dessert.

YIELDS: 16 servings
CORKY'S FAMILY: Zachary Pelts

2 large Granny Smith apples

2 (8-ounce) cans refrigerated crescent rolls

1 cup sugar

¾ cup (1½ sticks) unsalted butter

1 (12-ounce) can or bottle Mountain Dew soda

½ teaspoon cinnamon sugar

Preheat the oven to 350°F. Peel and core the apples, and cut each into 8 slices. Open the can of crescent rolls and lay out the dough. Roll 1 piece of apple in each triangle of dough, beginning with large end. Place the dumplings in a 13 x 9-inch pan with high sides. In a heavy-bottomed saucepan set over medium heat, melt the sugar and butter. Pour the butter mixture over the crescent rolls and follow with the Mountain Dew. (The recipe can be prepared ahead of time; cover and refrigerate until ready to bake.) Sprinkle dumplings with cinnamon sugar and bake until sauce is bubbling and the dough is cooked through, about 45 minutes.

NANCY'S BLACKBERRY COBBLER

Blackberry and peach cobblers are staples in the South. This quick and easy cobbler is just as tasty with blueberries or raspberries if you so choose.

YIELDS: 6 to 8 servings
CORKY'S FRIEND: Nancy Bynon

5 cups fresh blackberries, washed and drained

1 cup all-purpose flour

1 cup sugar

1 teaspoon baking powder

¾ teaspoon salt

1 medium egg, beaten

½ cup (1 stick) unsalted butter, melted

¼ teaspoon ground cinnamon

Vanilla ice cream *(for serving)*

Preheat the oven to 350°F. Arrange the blackberries evenly in a 2-quart baking dish. Combine the flour, sugar, baking powder, and salt in a bowl and mix well. Stir in the egg and crumble the mixture over the berries. Drizzle with the melted butter and sprinkle with the cinnamon. Bake until topping is golden brown and filling bubbles, about 45 minutes. Serve warm, topped with vanilla ice cream.

UNCLE ANDY'S PEACH COBBLER*

YIELDS: 10 servings
CORKY'S FAMILY: Andy Woodman

½ cup (1 stick) unsalted butter, melted

2 cups sugar, divided

1 cup all-purpose flour

1 tablespoon baking powder

Pinch of salt

1 cup milk

4 cups peeled and sliced peaches *(from about 5 to 6 medium peaches)*

1 tablespoon freshly squeezed lemon juice

1 teaspoon cinnamon sugar

Preheat the oven to 375°F. Pour the melted butter into a 13 x 9-inch baking dish. Combine 1 cup of the sugar, flour, baking powder, and salt in a large bowl, stirring to combine. Add the milk and stir until the dry ingredients are moistened. Pour the batter into the baking dish.

Combine the remaining 1 cup of sugar, peach slices, and lemon juice in a heavy saucepan over high heat; bring to a boil, stirring constantly. Remove from the heat and pour the peaches over the batter (do not stir into the batter).

Bake until dough is golden brown and peach juices bubble, about 40 to 45 minutes. Sprinkle the top with cinnamon sugar and serve warm or cold.

✱ *Peach cobbler is one of the most requested desserts in the restaurant. It's no wonder—there's little that tastes better than ripe peaches, warm and sweet, with a buttery dough.*

MISS BETTY'S CARAMEL CAKE

Miss Betty has been taking care of Corky's customers for as long as we can remember. She's also Don Pelts' sister-in-law. (We like family around here. Have you figured that out yet?) Her Southern caramel cake is requested for both family and work get-togethers. It is a little labor-intensive, but we assure you, your efforts will be worth it. Don't be surprised if this cake becomes a must-have request from your friends and family.

YIELDS: 8 servings

CORKY'S FAMILY: Betty Pelts

Cake

Nonstick cooking spray, oil, or butter

1 cup (2 sticks) margarine, softened

½ cup vegetable shortening *(Crisco preferred)*

3 cups sugar

6 large eggs

3 cups cake flour, sifted, plus additional for pans

1 cup milk

1 teaspoon vanilla extract

Icing

1 cup buttermilk

½ cup (1 stick) margarine

¼ teaspoon vanilla extract

3 cups sugar, divided

For cake: Preheat the oven to 350°F. Using nonstick spray, oil, or butter, grease and flour four 8-inch cake pans or one tube pan. Using an electric mixer, cream together the margarine and shortening and then add the sugar, a little at a time, mixing between additions. Add the eggs and continue mixing. Add the 3 cups of flour and milk in batches, mixing between additions and alternating between dry and wet ingredients. Add the vanilla and mix to blend. Pour the batter into the prepared pans and bake until a toothpick inserted comes out clean, about 20 to 25 minutes. If any of the layers are uneven after baking, cover the warm cake with a clean kitchen towel, and gently press on the domed areas to flatten. Cool the cakes in the pans for 10 minutes, and then remove from the pans onto a wire rack and let cool completely. While the cakes are cooling, make the icing.

For icing: Combine the buttermilk, margarine, vanilla extract, and 2½ cups of sugar in a heavy-bottomed saucepan over medium heat. In a separate heavy saucepan, add the remaining ½ cup of sugar and spread evenly over the bottom. Cook over medium heat and stir gently with a silicone spatula until the sugar browns, taking care not to burn. As soon as the sugar has browned, pour it into the saucepan with the other ingredients and continue to cook, stirring constantly, until the mixture reaches soft ball stage, approximately 235°F. (To test without a candy thermometer, drop a bit of the hot syrup in a bowl of cold water. If it has reached the soft ball stage, you'll be able to form the syrup into a ball in the cold water, but it will naturally flatten in your hand when you remove it

from the water.) Pour the icing into a glass or ceramic mixing bowl and allow to cool about 15 minutes. Using a handheld electric mixer, beat the icing until it reaches a spreadable consistency.

To ice the cake, place one cooled cake layer upside-down on a serving platter and pour a fifth of the icing over the top, spreading evenly. Carefully place the second layer upside-down on top of the bottom layer and spread another fifth of the icing over it. Repeat with the third layer. Place the fourth cake layer right-side up, spreading the remainder of the icing on the top and sides of the cake. (The icing cools and thickens quickly, so you may need to microwave the remaining icing in 25-second intervals, stirring between, until it returns to a spreadable consistency.) Let the cake stand for at least 2 hours before serving.

The finished cake freezes beautifully for up to one month. Freeze until the icing has hardened, then wrap tightly first in plastic wrap and then in foil before returning to the freezer. To thaw, leave all the wrapping intact and thaw in the refrigerator for 24 hours. Unwrap only after it's completely thawed to prevent weepy icing.

SIMPLY DELICIOUS STRAWBERRY CAKE

YIELDS: 8 servings

CORKY'S FAMILY: Tricia Woodman

Cake

Nonstick cooking spray, oil, or butter

All-purpose flour, for pans

1 (18.25-ounce) box white cake mix

1 (3-ounce) package strawberry gelatin mix *(Jell-O preferred)*

½ cup vegetable oil

½ cup water

½ cup puréed strawberries *(about 1 cup whole)*

4 large egg whites, at room temperature, beaten until stiff

Icing

1 (1-pound) box powdered sugar

½ cup (1 stick) unsalted butter, softened

½ cup puréed strawberries *(about 1 cup whole)*

To make the cake, preheat the oven to 350°F. Using nonstick spray, oil, or butter, grease and flour three 8-inch round cake pans or a 13 x 9-inch baking pan. In a large mixing bowl, combine the cake mix, gelatin mix, oil, and ½ cup of water and beat at medium speed until well-blended. Fold in the puréed strawberries and then carefully fold in the beaten egg whites. Divide batter among the prepared pans and bake until a toothpick inserted into the center of the cake comes out clean, about 30 to 40 minutes. If any of the layers are uneven after baking, cover the warm cake with a clean kitchen towel, and gently press on the domed areas to flatten. Cool the cakes in the pans for 10 minutes, and then remove from the pans onto a wire rack and let cool completely. While the cakes are cooling, make the icing.

For icing: Beat the powdered sugar, butter, and strawberries together at medium speed until well blended. To ice the layered cake, place one cooled cake layer upside-down on a serving platter and pour one-third of the icing over the top, spreading evenly. Carefully place the second layer right-side up on top of the bottom layer and spread another third of the icing over it. Spread the remainder of the icing on the sides of the cake. To ice a sheet cake, simply spread the icing evenly over the cooled cake.

MISSISSIPPI MUD CAKE

This rich, fudgy chocolate cake has a sticky, yummy marshmallow topping. Bring on the milk!

YIELDS: 18 to 20 servings

CORKY'S FRIEND: Jeannie Stevens Jones

Nonstick cooking spray, oil, or butter

2 cups sugar

1 cup (2 sticks) margarine, softened

3 tablespoons unsweetened cocoa powder

4 medium eggs

1 teaspoon vanilla extract

1½ cups all-purpose flour, plus additional for pan

1½ cups shredded dried coconut

1½ cups chopped nuts *(optional)*

1 (13-ounce) container marshmallow creme

1 (16-ounce) can chocolate frosting

Chocolate chips *(for garnish)*

To make the cake, preheat the oven to 350°F. Using nonstick cooking spray, oil, or butter, grease and flour a 13 x 9-inch baking pan. Using an electric mixer, cream together the sugar, margarine, and cocoa. Add the eggs and vanilla and mix well. Add in the 1½ cups flour, coconut, and nuts and mix well. Pour the batter into the prepared pan. Bake until a tester inserted into the center comes out clean, about 30 to 40 minutes.

While the cake is still warm, about 3 to 5 minutes after removing the cake from the oven, cover the cake with the marshmallow cream and immediately place tablespoonfuls of chocolate frosting in a random pattern over the marshmallow. Use a knife or spatula to swirl the toppings together in a marbled pattern. Refrigerate overnight. Garnish with chocolate chips.

EMMA'S CHOCOLATE CHIP COOKIES

YIELDS: 4 dozen 3-inch cookies

CORKY'S FAMILY: Emma Woodman

1 cup (2 sticks) unsalted butter, softened

¾ cup sugar

¾ cup firmly packed brown sugar

2 large eggs

1½ teaspoons vanilla extract

2¼ cups all-purpose flour

1 teaspoon baking soda

Pinch of salt

1½ cup semi-sweet chocolate chips

1 cup coarsely chopped walnuts or pecans *(optional)*

In a large mixing bowl, beat the butter until smooth. Add both types of sugar and beat for several minutes until fluffy. Beat in the eggs one at a time. Add the vanilla and beat until incorporated, scraping down the sides of the bowl as needed.

In a separate bowl, combine the flour, baking soda, and salt. Slowly add the dry ingredients to the egg mixture and beat until incorporated. Fold in the chocolate chips and nuts. Cover the dough and refrigerate for at least 30 minutes.

Preheat the oven to 375°F. Line baking sheets with parchment paper or silicone baking mats. Drop the dough by the tablespoonful onto the prepared baking sheets. Bake until the cookies are golden brown around the edges, about 10 to 12 minutes. Remove from the oven and allow to cool slightly before transferring to a wire rack.

Note: The dough can be frozen: Form balls and place on a lined baking sheet. Freeze completely and then store in a resealable plastic bag in the freezer. When ready to bake, simply place the frozen dough balls on a baking sheet and bake as directed, increasing baking time by two minutes.

WHOOPIE PIES

Kids love to make—and eat—these fluffy cookies stuffed with marshmallow cream.

YIELDS: 12 large or 24 small pies

CORKY'S FRIEND: Mary Roberts

Filling

1 (13-ounce) container marshmallow creme

½ cup (1 stick) unsalted butter, softened

1 cup powdered sugar

1 teaspoon vanilla extract

Cakes

1 (18.25-ounce) box devil's food cake mix *(Duncan Hines preferred)*

1 (3.9-ounce) box instant chocolate pudding mix

3 large eggs

⅓ cup vegetable oil

¾ cup water

For filling: In medium bowl, mix together the marshmallow cream and butter. Add the sugar and vanilla and mix well. Place in the refrigerator to set while the cakes are baking and cooling.

For cakes: Preheat the oven to 350°F. Line baking sheets with parchment paper. In large bowl, whisk all of the ingredients together. Drop batter by equal-sized, rounded scoopfuls onto the paper. Bake until set, about 10 minutes. Allow to cool completely before filling.

Assemble the pies by spreading the filling onto the flat side of half of the cakes and topping with the remaining cakes. Let set in the refrigerator before serving.

SUGAR NUT PASTRIES

These little cookies absolutely melt in your mouth.

YIELDS: 36 servings

CORKY'S FAMILY: Bryna Woodman

1 cup (2 sticks) unsalted butter, softened

¼ cup powdered sugar, plus additional for coating the pastries

2 cups all-purpose flour

1 teaspoon vanilla extract

½ teaspoon salt

1 cup chopped pecans

Cream the butter and ¼ cup sugar together in a mixer. Add the flour, vanilla, and salt and beat to combine. Stir in the chopped pecans. Chill the dough, covered, for at least 30 minutes.

Preheat the oven to 300°F. Line baking sheets with parchment paper. Form the dough into walnut-sized balls and place on the baking sheets. Bake until golden brown, about 20 to 25 minutes. While the pastries are still warm, roll them in powdered sugar.

AMIR'S BANANAS FOSTER

YIELDS: 4 servings

CORKY'S FAMILY: Amir Abdol

¼ cup (½ stick) unsalted butter

½ cup firmly packed dark brown sugar

½ teaspoon ground cinnamon

¼ cup banana liqueur

4 bananas *(not over-ripe)*

¼ cup dark rum

Ice cream *(for serving)*

Chopped pecans *(for serving)*

Melt the butter in a heavy, 10-inch skillet over low heat. Add the brown sugar and cinnamon and mix well, heating until the sugar dissolves. Add the banana liqueur and bring the sauce to a simmer. Add the whole bananas and cook for 1 minute each side, carefully spooning the sauce over the bananas as they cook. Using a slotted spoon, remove the bananas from the pan and place each in a serving dish. Bring the sauce back to a simmer and carefully add the rum. If the sauce is very hot, the rum will flame on its own. If not, use a long match or lighter and carefully ignite the sauce. Continue cooking until the flame dies out, usually 1 to 2 minutes. If the sauce is too thin, cook for an additional 1 to 2 minutes for a syrupy consistency. Spoon the sauce over the bananas and serve immediately with ice cream and chopped pecans.

Any holiday weekend or Memphis in May, you'll find Don (Corky's founder) and me down on the river selling barbecue. If the restaurant's busy, we may be bussing tables or hosting. Tomorrow we'll all be working a big catering gig. We're definitely entrenched in the running of things. Corky's is a true family business, and I think the employees appreciate that.

— Andy Woodman, co-owner of Corky's

ASHLEY'S BANANA PUDDING

The Corky's clan always serves this banana pudding with Momo's Hot Fudge Sauce. Remember, everything tastes better with Momo's—and banana pudding is no exception. Have fun with your serving dishes, too. You can make this in a pretty bowl or use small dishes for individual servings. We opted for mason-jar wine glasses. If you can't use those for banana pudding, when can you?

YIELDS: 6 to 8 servings

CORKY'S FRIEND: Ashley Baker

1 (3.4-ounce) package instant vanilla pudding mix

3 cups whole milk

1 (14-ounce) can sweetened condensed milk

1 (12-ounce) container whipped topping

1 (12-ounce) box vanilla wafers

6 bananas, peeled and sliced

1 recipe Momo's Hot Fudge Sauce (page 202) *(optional, for serving)*

In a large bowl, combine the pudding, milk, sweetened condensed milk, and whipped topping. Crush 10 wafers in a small bowl and set aside. In a serving dish layer the ingredients beginning with the whole vanilla wafers, the bananas, and then the pudding mixture. Repeat with as many layers as your bowl allows and top with wafer crumbs. Cover and chill in the refrigerator until ready to serve. Top with Momo's Hot Fudge Sauce, if desired.

I've been a vegetarian since 1994. I don't fall off the vegetarian wagon except when I go to Memphis and eat at Corky's. The last time I went there, it was a 6000 mile road trip for the sole purpose of ribs, onion loaf, tamales, and—of course—sweet tea. The owner got wind that this crazy girl and her grandmother loved Corky's enough to drive cross-country for some pork, so he sent my grandmother a care package to her new home in Oregon. She ended up with this amazing, comforting, taste-of-home meal—complete with a southern pecan pie. Nothing in this world could've made her happier.

— Miki Markovich, *far-flung fan of Corky's*

BLUEBERRY BREAD PUDDING WITH WHITE CHOCOLATE SAUCE

This recipe won the cook-off in our test kitchen against a blueberry cake doughnut bread pudding. The croissants in the bread pudding give it a beautiful, buttery flavor and texture. Try it with both sauces—the lemon drizzle on the cake doughnut version was so good, we had to include the recipe, too.

YIELDS: 10 to 12 servings

CORKY'S FAMILY: Sheila Thomas and Jimmy Stovall

Nonstick cooking spray, oil, or butter

6 to 8 large croissants

6 large eggs

1 cup sugar

1 cup sweetened condensed milk

2 tablespoons vanilla extract

2 cups fresh or frozen blueberries

½ cup pecan pieces

3 cups white chocolate chips

½ cup (1 stick) unsalted butter

3 tablespoons whiskey *(optional)*

Preheat the oven to 350°F. Using nonstick spray, oil, or butter, grease a 13 x 9-inch baking dish. Tear the croissants into pieces and spread over the bottom of the prepared dish. In a large bowl, combine the eggs, sugar, sweetened condensed milk, and vanilla. Whisk to blend well, and then pour the mixture evenly over the croissants. Sprinkle the blueberries and pecans over the top and bake until pudding is puffed, golden and set, about 50 minutes. Let cool slightly on a wire rack.

To make the white chocolate sauce, combine the white chocolate chips and butter in the top of a double boiler over simmering water. Cook until the mixture is melted and smooth, whisking constantly. (The butter and white chocolate chips can also be melted in the microwave. Microwave on high, uncovered, in 30-seconds intervals, stirring between. Repeat until the chocolate chips are completely melted and smooth.) Stir in the whiskey, if using, just before serving.

Serve the bread pudding with the sauce over the top or on the side. For a twist, try the Lemon Sauce (recipe follows) instead. It pairs wonderfully with the blueberries. Both sauces can be prepared ahead and stored in a covered container in the refrigerator. To serve, heat in the microwave in 25-second intervals, stirring between, until the consistency is right for pouring.

JIMMY'S LEMON SAUCE

YIELDS: 10 to 12 servings

CORKY'S FAMILY: Jimmy Stovall

2 cups powdered sugar

½ cup (1 stick) unsalted butter, melted

2 tablespoons freshly squeezed lemon juice *(from about ½ lemon)*

1 teaspoon vanilla extract

Combine all the ingredients and mix well until completely smooth. (Can be prepared ahead of time. Cover and refrigerate the sauce until ready to use. To serve, heat in the microwave at 25 second intervals, stirring until the consistency is right for pouring.) Drizzle over the Blueberry Bread Pudding.

HOMEMADE VANILLA OR PEACH ICE CREAM

"Growing up in the South, homemade ice cream was a part of every summer gathering. We would often have several batches going at the same time," says Sheila. "I remember my brother and I taking turns sitting on the crank freezers while Grandpa and Uncle Huey turned the crank. The creamy scoops of vanilla were worth all the effort on those hot summer nights. With all of the electric ice cream freezers available these days, making homemade ice cream is certainly easier on the derrière, and the end result tastes just as creamy and delicious."

YIELDS: 4 quarts

CORKY'S FAMILY: Sheila Thomas

3 cups whole milk

1¾ cup sugar

½ teaspoon salt

2 cups half-and-half

1 tablespoon vanilla extract

3 cups heavy whipping cream

3 to 4 cups fresh peach purée *(optional)*

Heat the milk in a medium saucepan over medium heat until bubbles begin to form around the edge of the pan. Watch carefully, making sure not to let the milk boil or scald.

Remove from the heat and add the sugar and salt, stirring until dissolved. Stir in the half-and-half, vanilla, and whipping cream. If making peach ice cream, stir in the fresh peaches. Cover and refrigerate for at least 30 minutes, or until the mixture has cooled completely.

Freeze in your ice cream machine according to the manufacturer's directions.

ZOE'S BLACKBERRY SORBET

Don't skip the vodka—it helps minimize the crystallization and gives the sorbet its creamy texture, which is almost like a fruit gelato.

YIELDS: 6 to 8 servings

CORKY'S FAMILY: Zoe Pelts

2½ cups fresh blackberries (about 18 ounces), washed and drained

½ cup water

1¼ cups sugar

2 tablespoons freshly squeezed lemon juice *(from about ½ lemon)*

1 tablespoon vodka

In a blender, purée the blackberries with ½ cup of water until smooth. Strain through a fine-mesh sieve to remove all of the seeds. Discard the seeds and transfer the berry mixture to a stainless steel bowl. Add the sugar, lemon juice, and vodka to the blackberry mixture and set the bowl in an ice bath or in the refrigerator to chill the mixture before freezing. Stir occasionally until all of the sugar is dissolved.

Freeze the sorbet in your ice cream machine according to the manufacturer's instructions (it will be soft). Transfer the sorbet to an airtight container and freeze for several hours to harden into a scoopable consistency. The sorbet will keep for up to 1 week in the freezer.

Corky's, yes! Dry ribs, yes! Pecan pie, YES. The BF and I stopped in at Corky's on our Great American Road Trip 'cuz we heard that's where we could get the best BBQ. I'm no connoisseur, but yowza, that was some tasty Q. We almost forgot how deelishus the ribs and pulled pork were after we scarfed down a piece of hands-down-the-best-pecan-pie-I-have-had-in-my-whole-life. I will come back someday, Corky!

— *a review from Bevin, Cambridge, MA*

PEACH PARK MILKSHAKE

Memphians make a habit of summer beach vacations, with a favorite spot being Alabama's Gulf Coast. The road trip through southern Alabama is a long one, but the anticipation of a regular stop along I-65 at the Peach Park restaurant always makes the trip a little less painful. The Peach Park is located in Clanton, Alabama, and is home to the world's largest peach. This destination is the undisputed home of the best homemade peach ice cream ever, according to Brigadier General Brown, who challenged us to figure out their secret. They don't give out their prized recipe, but we whirred our blender through countless attempts at recreating our favorite milkshake. We think you'll like the results. Should you ever find yourself on I-65 in south Alabama, keep an eye out for the gigantic peach and be sure to stop. You'll be glad you did.

YIELDS: 2 servings

CORKY'S FRIEND: David Brown

1 cup sliced fresh peaches
(from about 2 peaches)

¼ cup pineapple juice

¼ cup sugar

2 cups vanilla ice cream
(preferably homemade)

¾ cup whole milk

In a blender, purée the peaches, pineapple juice, and sugar until smooth. Add the ice cream and blend until smooth. Pour in the milk and blend well. Pour into chilled glasses, add straws, and enjoy.

> I'm embarrassed at my behavior. Thank goodness it was in my hotel and not in public. Dry-rub ribs were a new thing for me, and I shamelessly put them away, one by one, until I was ready to pop. What side dishes? Who cares? I'm here for the ribs, man. Oh btw—they have a drive-through window, which is handy because the parking here is insane.
>
> — *a review from BS, Menlo Park, CA*

TOASTED MARSHMALLOW MILKSHAKE

For best results, have your ice cream and milk already in the blender while toasting the marshmallows, since the marshmallows will blend better when still hot from the oven. Up the level from decadent to crazy-decadent by topping with Momo's Hot Fudge Sauce (page 202). Remember, everything's better with Momo's!

YIELDS: 4 servings

CORKY'S FAMILY: Carol Sweeney

2 cups vanilla ice cream

1½ cups whole milk

1 (16-ounce) bag jumbo marshmallows

Momo's Hot Fudge Sauce
(page 202—for serving; optional)

Preheat the broiler and line a baking sheet with parchment paper. Arrange all but 4 of the marshmallows on the prepared baking sheet in a single layer. Put the ice cream and milk into the blender in preparation for the toasted marshmallows. Broil the marshmallows, turning each once or twice and watching carefully, until the marshmallows are completely charred, about 2 minutes. Add the toasted marshmallows to the milk and ice cream in the blender. Blend until well combined, about 3 minutes.

To serve, toast the remaining 4 marshmallows under the broiler until slightly golden. Pour the milkshake mixture into 4 (8-ounce) glasses and garnish each with a toasted marshmallow. Top with hot fudge sauce, if desired, and serve.

CONTRIBUTING FAMILY, FRIENDS, & FAR-FLUNG FANS

INDEX

Cookin' with Corky's: Dig in with family and friends from Memphis' legendary Bar-B-Q joint!

Jimmy Stovall *with* Andy Woodman *and* Barry Pelts

Library of Congress Control Number: 2013934619

ISBN-13: 978-0-87197-577-5 (print)

ISBN-13: 978-0-87197-578-2 (eBook)

Published and distributed by Favorite Recipes Press
an imprint of Southwestern Publishing Group, Inc.

www.frpbooks.com | www.swpublishinggroup.com

P. O. Box 305142, Nashville Tennessee 37230 | 1-800-358-0560

For information on Corky's, visit CorkysBBQ.com.

Project Manager: Sheila Thomas

Test Kitchen Manager: Carol Sweeney

Editing and design by Terrace Partners

Hand-lettering and illustrations by Lee Newton (figleef.com)

Select photographs on endsheets and p. 4 by John Sharman

Select photographs on endsheets by Caylan Vanaman

Select photographs pgs. 17, 18, 28, 32-33 by Mike Stanton

Vintage photographs from Corky's private collection

Food photography by Jay Adkins (jayadkinsphotography.com)

Food styling by Julia Rutland, Sheila Thomas, and Jimmy Stovall

Manufactured in the USA

10 9 8 7 6 5 4 3 2 1